The Art & Science of
PATTERNING
WHITETAILS

Dr. James C. Kroll

Director, Institute for White-tailed Deer
          Management and Research, and
Professor, College of Forestry
Stephen F. Austin State University
Nacogdoches, Texas

Gordon Whittington

Editor, **North American WHITETAIL** Magazine
Marietta, Georgia

With photography by **Mike Biggs**

A Center for Applied Studies in Forestry Publication

Second Edition
2 3 4 5 6 7 8 9

ISBN 0-938361-19-8

Publication also supported by:
Temple-Inland Inc.
Game & Fish Publications
North American WHITETAIL Magazine

Acknowledgments

As best hunting buddies, we have spanned North America in our quest for quality whitetails. We have sat high atop spruce trees in New Brunswick and have hidden behind logs in southwestern Missouri, trying to take an elusive trophy. Sometimes we have won and sometimes we have lost the mental battle with these wonderful creatures. But, win or lose, our success has not been measured by the number of trophies on our walls. It is measured by the number of great experiences and fine friends we have enjoyed over the years. Therefore, we would like to thank the following people for all they have done for us and the white-tailed deer:

Ken Bailey, Scott Beasley, Steve Bentsen, Terry Birkholz, Randy Browning, James and Beth Bullard, Mark Buxton, Dave Bzawy, Bill Carter, George and Paul Chase, H. H. Coffield Estate, Mark Conway, Jack Cooper, Mark Cooper, Debbie Corbin, Scott Dahler, Amos DeWitt, Paul and Skipper Dickson, Jon Ducharme, Bob and Mark Ellett, John Finegan, David Guynn, Randy Ivy, Harry Jacobson, Ray Knight, Ben Koerth, Jim McAllen, David Morris, Bobby Parker Jr., Tonya Sheffield, Phil Smart, Jerry and Julie Stafford, Kenneth Sutton, Steve Vaughn, Louisa Vaughn, Steve Warner, Larry Weishuhn, Terry Westmoreland, David Whitehouse, John Wootters, all our friends who let us use their photos in our book, and the countless others who have helped in various ways.

This book would be far less without the photography of Mike Biggs! He truly is one of the very best. If you share our appreciation for his work, you might want to purchase a copy of his full-color book, **Amazing Whitetails**. It is an excellent way to learn about deer behavior.

We both owe our careers to the white-tailed deer. We never cease to marvel at their adaptability, especially in the face of growing human populations.

CONTENTS

Chapters

CHAPTER 1

What is Patterning?

Since prehistoric times, man the predator has pitted his highly evolved brain against the superior physical abilities of various prey species, in a chess match with life-and-death consequences. Once humans began to stalk food with the capacity to outrun them, they found themselves at a serious athletic disadvantage; only those who used their cerebral edge lived long enough to stay in the game. The most successful human predators learned to study their quarry and the habitat in which those animals lived, then come up with plans to make regular kills — to be, for lack of a better way to put it, "in the right place at the right time." In other words, they learned to *pattern* prey or risk going hungry in a hostile world.

Being "in the right place at the right time" is just as beneficial to today's deer hunter as it was to the cave

The authors — Gordon (left) and James — show off two mature bucks from the Glass Ranch in South Texas.

dwellers of 20,000 years ago. OK, maybe the stakes aren't as high for us — we do, after all, have other options for procuring our next meal — but the task is viewed just as seriously today as it was back then. Today's advanced hunter knows quite well that staying one step ahead of the game is the only way to enjoy consistent success. And in perhaps no other type of hunting is that as necessary, or as challenging, as when pursuing the white-tailed deer.

Today, much is written about "patterning;" yet, most hunters' knowledge of this process continues to lag far behind their enthusiasm for deer hunting. Patterning a deer sounds mysterious, and many modern hunters frankly fear they lack what is required to get the job done. So, increasing numbers of today's deer hunters choose instead to keep grabbing at every hot new product that comes down the pike, hoping to hit upon a success formula that requires no investment in time, perspiration or brainpower. Short on free hours in which to pursue their sport, and no longer living close enough to the land to pick up much hunting savvy on a daily basis, these outdoorsmen are indeed a curious paradox. They continue to look to the future to bring them "breakthrough" developments that will foster success, even as they are being swept farther and farther from the skills that will give them what they want most from deer hunting.

We, the authors of this book, understand all too well that free time is limited and that not everyone has a high-quality deer herd at their disposal. Most of you reading these words are already somewhat successful in your whitetail hunting, but feel your capacity for improvement is limited. You hope to become an increasingly more consistent harvester of deer — especially mature bucks — but somehow find yourself unable to take those last few critical steps.

We are happy to report that the methods outlined in this book can help you do just that. Whether you have shot 100 deer or have yet to notch your first tag, you can learn a lot from what is in the chapters that follow. And, it does not matter whether you live in central Pennsylvania or eastern Montana or northern Alabama; it does not even matter whether you consider yourself a "trophy" hunter, a "meat" hunter or something in between. A whitetail is a whitetail, and our proven strategy for patterning these noble animals will work anywhere they are found.

In one important sense, this book promises to go beyond the scope of some other how-to volumes. Many other deer-hunting books focus strictly on the personal experiences of the author, serving almost as a diary of his hunting career. If your own hunting terrain and/or hunting style closely resembles that of the author, you can in fact learn a great deal from what he has to say. However, if you feel your deer-hunting situation is far different from his, you might find yourself questioning whether or not his strategies will work for you, where you hunt.

Patterning big bucks like this really involves little more than spending your time in the woods wisely.

Our combined backgrounds and professions have afforded us the rare opportunity to produce a book which we are quite confident will help deer hunters everywhere. James has hunted whitetails since childhood and for many years has served as Director of the Institute for White-tailed Deer Management and Research, in Nacogdoches, Texas. He also has been a widely published author on a variety of whitetail topics in both the popular and academic press, and is among the most respected deer biologists and seminar speakers in the world. Gordon likewise grew up in a deer stand and for more than a decade has served as editor of **North American WHITETAIL** magazine, the world's largest-circulation deer publication. Along the way, we have hunted, both together and separately, from one end of the continent's deer country to the other, and we have established a network of contacts that is second to none. Thus, it is with complete confidence that we say this book can help you become an even better deer hunter, no matter where you live or how much time you have to hunt.

That we were writing a book on patterning created quite a stir among whitetail hunters; finally someone was going to address the most confusing aspect of hunting. Yet, in talking with folks about our book, we became concerned that there is much confusion as to exactly what patterning is. Some guys think it is knowing precisely when a particular buck is going to walk past a specific oak tree — not so! Years of research and experience on our part has taught us a valuable lesson. James' research, for example, on deer movements and activity patterns yielded many of the answers regarding what makes deer tick. But, the one thing it has not given up is *when* a buck is going to appear. And, it probably never will. Patterning is *not* about knowing what a specific animal is going to do at a specific point in time. Rather, it is learning about habitat preferences, feeding patterns and strategies, reproductive cycles and behavior of deer living in a specific place. That's what this book is about.

Patterning whitetails, as you soon will learn, is really little more than spending your time in the woods wisely, and then applying common sense to make accurate predictions about overall deer movement. There are other ways to define the process, but for our purposes, this one serves well enough. By employing our methods, you quickly will learn to study your hunting area without leaving the comforts of your home, so that you can maximize the productivity of your actual field time. You will learn to recognize deer sign better than ever before, so you not only can locate deer areas, but determine exactly how they are being used. You will learn to understand the connections between where deer hide and feed and breed, and you will see how to make those connections work in your favor as a hunter, You will begin to feel the land and its subtle rhythms in a new way, to truly become a part of the woods. As a result, you not only will gain a greater knowledge of deer hunting, but will find greater satisfaction in it as well.

Neither of us can guarantee you that reading this book will automatically allow you to fill every deer tag or put a monster buck on your wall each year. But if you study the pages that follow, and apply what is written in them, we *will* guarantee you can improve your odds of not only harvesting the kind of deer you want, but also of enjoying your precious time in the woods even more. And as you climb into your deer stand on opening morning, that is about as good a feeling as any hunter can have.

CHAPTER 2

Basic Deer Biology

As was pointed out in the previous chapter, primitive man was a skilled hunter, relying on great knowledge of the behavior and habitat preferences of his quarry in order to survive. By contrast, many modern hunters know little about the biology and behavior of game. In order to effectively pattern whitetail movements, and then arrive at a successful strategy, the hunter must fully understand what the local deer are doing, and why.

This chapter will serve as a primer to the aspects of whitetail biology we feel are most important to patterning. Deer biology is a complex subject (see James' book, **A Practical Guide to Producing and Harvesting White-tailed Deer**, for a more in-depth discussion), but here we will examine only those aspects that relate directly to patterning.

Deer Social Biology

The basic social unit of whitetails is the *family group*, also called the *matriarchal unit*. It is made up of two or more individuals, most of which are genetically related. Family group size varies, depending on geography and population density. For example, a family group in Saskatchewan might consist only of one doe and her female offspring, while a typical group in Alabama might contain 20 or more individuals.

Bucks also organize into social groups, ranging from two to a dozen males. Unlike doe groups, buck social groups normally are *not* composed entirely of related individuals. To the contrary, bucks tend to become socialized either by accidental associations or as a result of "friendships" established as fawns.

During the velvet stage, bucks often form bachelor groups, with their activities centered around prime feeding areas. These groups always disband as the pre-rut approaches.

Within each social unit, male or female, there exists a hierarchy of individuals. Matriarchal groups are so called because there is a matriarch, a dominant ("alpha") doe that pretty much runs the show. Most of the research we have conducted indicates that these "alpha" does are from three to perhaps five years of age. Younger does usually lack the experience to become dominant within a group, and does older than age five years often lack the physical ability to hold onto their position.

As an example, let's consider the case of an East Texas doe that was radio-collared and tracked over her entire adult life. She became dominant at age 3 1/2 and remained so for two years. The second doe in the group's hierarchy (the "beta" doe) was one of her first daughters. Together, the two of them decided what the entire group would do and when they would do it. Any deer that did not follow their lead was dealt with harshly, through physical intimidation and kicks. This went on until the summer of the "alpha" doe's sixth year, when she suddenly left the group and established a new home range well away from that of her family group. She had lost her social position to her daughter, the former "beta" doe, which essentially had run her off from the group. How is that for family loyalty?

The size of doe social groups is directly related to the population density in the area and what stage of the growth cycle the population is in. Whitetails are quite adept at taking advantage of sudden improvements in forage conditions, such as an increase in browse following a tornado, clearcutting of mature timber or even climatic cycles. In most cases, deer populations grow to saturate their range in five to seven years following habitat improvement.

Dominant does occupy the best habitats and thus rear more fawns successfully.

Under low-population conditions, there are few doe social groups, and they are fairly small. As reproductive success increases, however, doe groups swell to maximum size. Increased social pressures within the group then force subordinate does to leave, searching for unoccupied habitat nearby. If all the available habitat is taken, the group remains relatively stable in size, because only the high-ranking does successfully rear their young. The "alpha" doe claims the best fawning territory, while the "beta" doe takes second best, and so on. Only during years of very good habitat conditions are subordinate does able to successfully rear fawns in densely populated areas.

Bucks spend their first year within the protective framework of the matriarchal group. But come early summer — when the buck is right at a year old — he suddenly becomes a social outcast and is driven from the group by his mother. As a result, the fawning season is a time of not only birth but of relocation as well, for these year-old bucks are roaming the countryside, looking for unoccupied habitat in which to establish themselves. This is a time of high mortality among young bucks, as they find themselves in unfamiliar surroundings filled with unknown dangers.

During this migration, young bucks start associating with others like themselves, forming "friendships" lasting throughout their lives — however long or short they might prove to be. We put quotation marks around the word "friendship" because it is not that type of relationship in the truest sense; rather, it is more of a mutually beneficial arrangement among the various individuals.

There are two types of buck social groups. The first is

Not all buck fights occur during the rut. Social dominance is gained primarily during the summer antler-growing season, when bucks use hooves instead of antlers in combat.

quite dynamic, made up of males only loosely associated with each other. There might be two or three bucks in the group this week, a larger number later. We refer to such groups as *federations*. The second type is the *friendship group*, which includes a dominant buck and one or more subordinates. These tend to be more permanent — except during the rut, when all social organization is suspended.

The dominant buck has a unique relationship to his subordinates. As bucks age, they feel less and less need to settle issues of social position. Each buck knows just where he stands in the "pecking order" and only tries to improve his position when the dominant buck is no longer around or when the "boss" becomes physically unable to continue dominance. In these friendship groups, the dominant buck plays the role of the western hero, while the subordinate is his sidekick. We have come to call the lesser buck in such relationships the "toady," which is derived from an old term that means a "flatterer."

Roy Carper passed up several small bucks before taking this West Virginia bruiser in 1986.

Both the dominant buck and his subordinate(s) benefit from such a relationship. Although the "toady" is not dominant, he gets to enjoy some of his dominant companion's social benefits. (Breeding rights are a notable exception.) Also, the subordinate buck often is younger than the dominant buck, and thus he learns by association. Once the dominant buck is no longer around, the "toady" can move more easily into a position of dominance

Dominant does, though smaller of body, can intimidate even mature bucks. Outside the breeding season, bucks generally yield the prime feeding areas to doe family groups.

himself.

Often it is the "toady," rather than the dominant animal, that is taken by the hunter. This generally is because the subordinate is less cautious than the older buck. A hunter commonly will work hard to pattern a buck, based strictly on sign interpretation, and then kill the "toady" as he works that pattern. In many cases, the *real* trophy buck was also close at hand, but was never even seen by the hunter. Often, the hunter never even knows he has shot the "wrong" animal, thinking he has taken the best buck.

James once was asked to show two young hunters how to pattern bucks in the National Forests of Texas, a heavily hunted public area. He patterned a nice buck and took the young men to the area he thought would be the best place to ambush the animal. "Whatever you do," he admonished, "don't shoot the first buck." He knew there must be a "toady" involved. At 15 minutes after first shooting light, one of the hunters shot the "toady!" Climbing down from his ladder stand, the hunter turned to look right into the eyes of the big buck, which got away unscathed.

For most of the year, buck and doe groups remain isolated from each other. Even when they use the same feeding areas in the summer, they tend to keep to themselves. At such times, it is not uncommon to see "alpha" does intimidating even the largest bucks on the feeding grounds. There is actually a good reason for this. Long ago, biologists learned that in many animal species, the male is the most expendable individual in the population. He is responsible only for maintaining the flow of genes, so that populations do not become inbred. Thus, males tend to be more mobile than are females in almost every animal species. This, along with a distinct breeding season in which males battle for dominance, results in a rela-

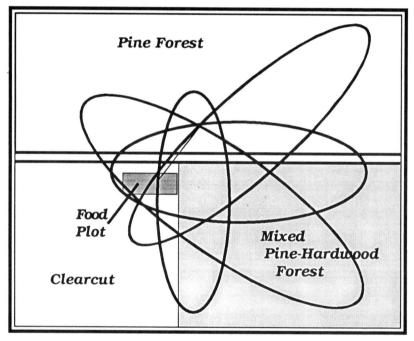

Although a number of doe groups may share the same feeding area, such as the food plot in this actual East Texas study, each group will have its own, distinct home range. These ranges almost always are elliptical in shape.

tively high natural mortality rate for males.

Outside of the breeding season, males have it harder than females do, because females tend to stake claim to the best habitats. The name of the game in nature is to successfully pass on your genes to the next generation, so males instinctively allow the females to have the best habitats in which to rear their young. Whitetail bucks thus tend to be in poorer habitats than do the does, especially in the spring and summer.

The feeding ground is the focus of social activity during much of the growing season. This could be an alfalfa field in Alberta, a soybean field in South Carolina or a two- year-old clearcut in Pennsylvania. Feeding grounds tend to influence the distribution of social groups. Because deer home ranges usually are elliptical in shape, a feeding ground can be the focal point for many social groups, all radiating out in various directions from that center.

These are areas of intense social interaction, for there are frequent opportunities for unfamiliar social groups to interact with each other. When a question of feeding "rights" arises, it is the "alpha" does in each group that settle the dispute. Rearing up on their hind legs, they flail at each other with their sharp front hooves, often landing serious blows. We have seen yearling bucks with antlers nearly torn from their heads by the hooves of irate does.

Feeding grounds also are dynamic. Whitetails seem to conduct a "moving party" in regard to feeding areas; they might concentrate their activity on one field for a week or more, then, for no apparent reason, suddenly shift all feeding to another spot some distance away. But in truth, there is a reason such shifts occur, and examination of the area in question often will reveal it.

Food sources such as agricultural crops can go from being highly nutritious to low in quality quite rapidly. Soybeans are a good example. A soybean plant is most attractive to deer during its early stages of growth. As the plant matures, however, it becomes covered with fine hairs that make it less attractive to deer. Also, nutritional composition changes. Whitetails even can detect differences in mineral content of certain plants, it seems. And

finally, deer simply might have an innate tendency to move about their range, no matter what the condition of the available forage, to allow browsed plants to recover. Whatever the reason(s) for the shift, you as a hunter certainly must be aware of it and plan your hunting accordingly.

Adjacent to every feeding area are distinct gathering places known as *staging areas.* These normally are located on the side of the food source that is downwind when the prevailing winds are blowing.

Fresh rubs and scrapes near a field edge revealed the staging area of this Iowa trophy buck.

A staging area usually is characterized by dense overhead cover (a thick canopy) with good visibility in the understory itself. These places even occur in big-woods country, along the interface between areas of heavy undergrowth and foraging areas, such as windfall timber or hardwood bottoms.

The purpose of the staging area is to give the deer a place to congregate prior to venturing out into the feeding ground. After any social disputes have been settled, the "alpha" doe generally leads the doe group onto the feeding ground itself. By contrast, when a buck social group enters the feeding area, the dominant buck rarely takes the lead position, preferring instead to lag behind his associates. (This helps to explain why a hunter who hasn't visually

identified the buck he's hunting sometimes ends up shooting the "wrong" buck while the biggest deer is still holding
in nearby cover.)

For example, consider the great buck shown on the
opposite page. This 184 5/8-point Pope and Young monster was shot in conjunction with a staging area on the edge
of a picked corn field in western Iowa on November 6, 1989.
Bowhunter Pat Salmen had only minutes before passed up
a basket-racked 8-pointer when he saw this non-typical
approaching. Pat's patience was rewarded with one of the
most impressive bucks you'll ever see.

It is the staging area which becomes the place of social
focus just prior to and during the rut. We will be looking at
such areas in much detail later.

Breeding Biology

As noted, normal whitetail behavior centers around a
dominance hierarchy, with well-defined social positions for
all animals in the group. Unfortunately, in many areas this
natural social system has broken down and no longer
holds true, due to skewed sex ratios stemming from the
overharvest of bucks. In many geographic areas, as many
as 70% of the bucks are harvested each hunting season,
leaving a scarcity of mature bucks and an unnatural
breeding biology in which immature males do most of the
breeding. It is important for you to know whether or not this
is true in your area, as it will greatly affect your hunting
strategy. Even with such problems, a basic knowledge of
deer breeding behavior will significantly improve your
ability to pattern deer for hunting purposes.

Whitetails are forest-dwelling animals by nature. Although they now are found in many states and provinces
that feature prairies and other "open" habitats, the traditional range and habitat of the whitetail was the forest. We
feel reasonably certain that the original population density
was quite low, especially before even the earliest native

Flehmen (lip curl) is a stereotypic behavior of male hoofed mammals. Using his tongue, the buck places scent on the roof of his mouth, so that it can be "smelled" by the Jacobson's organ. This behavior helps the buck to time his reproductive readiness to that of the does in his area.

peoples settled on this continent.

A forested environment in which sight is limited dictates that an animal must develop some other means of communication — particularly when the population density is low. While there are various ways in which animals can communicate their reproductive readiness to other members of the population, whitetails have "chosen" to rely upon chemicals.

The reproductive biology of many mammals, including deer, is controlled by chemicals called *pheromones.* These elicit specific behaviors and control the reproductive readiness of both males and females. A good example is the well-known flehmen (lip curling) behavior of cattle and other hoofed mammals, including whitetails. The male licks the female's genitalia, tarsal glands or urine and then places the material on a small structure

Rub-urination is a behavior practiced year-round by both bucks and does.

on the roof of his mouth called the *Jacobson's organ.* Scientists originally believed that this action helps the male determine the reproductive condition of the female, but recent anatomical evidence shows that organ has no connection to the smell-detecting portion of the brain. Thus, many researchers now believe this behavior serves to prime the male's reproductive readiness to coincide with that of the female.

Whitetails communicate with each other by using an array of chemicals, which are produced by at least seven glands. The function(s) of each of these glands is not fully understood, but we do know there are at least four of major significance. Two of these — the tarsal (hock) and forehead glands — are of greatest importance to us in terms of patterning deer.

Tarsal glands are the "communications center" for deer behavior. Scents deposited on these glands serve a wide variety of functions, both for bucks and does.

The tarsal glands are the best known to the average deer hunter. These patches on the inside of each back knee are not glands *per se*, however; rather, they are long tufts of hair with a waxy coating. Bucks and does alike have tarsal glands, and each sex uses them for chemical communication.

The primary display of tarsal gland use is *rub-urination behavior*. This is accomplished by pulling the hind legs together beneath the hips and urinating in a manner that causes the fluid to run down the hind legs. The deer actually tries to get the urine to come into contact with the tarsal glands, which apparently helps to retain certain urine-borne odors. The tufts of hair also might serve to help "age" these materials, which could strengthen their odor. Each sex will rub-urinate, saturating the tarsal glands with urine.

Rub-urination is used in marking scrapes and signpost rubs, as well as when two unfamiliar deer encounter each other. (The latter is particularly common with does.) Although rub-urination occurs most commonly during the breeding season, it is not unusual to see it in both bucks and does through the remainder of the year as well.

The second area of interest is the forehead gland. Although not as noticeable as the tarsal glands, it serves an important function for bucks. Combined with chemicals from the tarsal glands, the secretions of the forehead gland are used to mark signposts. If you smell the forehead of a mature buck, you will detect a pungent odor, and upon touching the forehead you will notice that the hairs have a waxy texture. The buck deposits materials from the tarsal glands onto the forehead by rubbing his head beneath the hind legs, directly against the tarsals. A dominant buck frequently has two dark brown "marks" on each side of the forehead as a result of this behavior.

The secretions of the tarsal and forehead glands have two primary functions. In goats, male secretions serve to bring females into a state of receptiveness for breeding. In fact, it has been shown a piece of cloth which has been rubbed on a male goat's "beard" (an area of scent retention) can be used to prime a female goat, bringing her into estrus. We feel the forehead and tarsal glands have a similar function for whitetails. Secretions from these glands appear to not only make females receptive but also to suppress breeding behavior among subordinate bucks that encounter the scents.

The signpost is one of the places where the dominant buck in an area accomplishes these tasks. *Most often a signpost is a large rub, one on which the dominant buck regularly rubs his forehead and antlers.* However, smaller

Glands in the forehead of a dominant buck may produce chemicals that suppress reproduction in younger bucks.

rubs and even scrapes also can serve as signposts. The antlers obviously secrete no chemicals of their own, but they often are rubbed against the tarsal glands or are used to rake the ground in scrapes. In either way they can pick up scents, which then are deposited on signposts. It has been hypothesized that velvet antlers first evolved to serve scent communication functions, then secondarily developed into combat structures after the velvet shedding phenomenon developed.

Subordinate bucks have been observed licking signposts. Presumably this behavior serves as the mechanism through which dominant bucks suppress the breeding activity of their subordinates. While this has not been documented, most biologists now feel it is the case.

Signposts are strategically placed. They often are located in staging areas, where they will be encountered by does and others bucks. Again, these staging areas most often are located downwind of feeding areas. Other signposts can be found within a few yards of a dominant buck's *bedding area,* or *sanctuary.* (Testosterone, the male hormone, is at its highest level in a buck's system right after he wakes up, and he often will feel the urge to rub prior to

Although signposts are visited by a broad array of deer — both bucks and does — they are originated exclusively by dominant bucks. These specialized rubs are most often found in sanctuaries and staging areas. They are used strictly for scent and visual communication, not exercise.

leaving his bedding area.) Other strategic locations where signposts commonly are found include selected spots on the buck's normal travel route, including "boundary" or "territorial" scrapes.

Although a buck continues to use his sanctuary most of his life (unless unduly disturbed), he may shift his activity from one staging area to another. This explains why a signpost might be actively worked for awhile, then abandoned for the remainder of the breeding season or perhaps activated again during the second estrus cycle ("secondary" rut).

How many bucks will work a given signpost rub or scrape? That depends on various factors, but in our experience, a number of bucks generally will work each one. While subordinate bucks often will lick the signpost, other dominant bucks passing through the area may

Subordinate bucks often visit signposts, stopping to smell and even lick them. Does also may visit and mark these rubs.

work the tree or scrape, depositing their own individual scent. Even if the dominant buck in an area is killed or dies naturally, favored signposts often will continue to see use, sometimes for a number of years. The best signpost locations apparently are ancestral, generally as a result of favorable topography or cover or both.

We now know the doe plays just as much of a role in getting the sexes together as the buck. He actually expends little effort in the act of breeding, but she gets actively involved in the process of selecting a mate (assuming there are enough bucks in the area for her to have a choice). The doe is biologically "stuck" with the quality of the fawns that result from her choice of mates; if she picks the wrong one, from a biological viewpoint she will "waste" a year rearing them. For this reason, she will actively assess the quality of bucks available to her and will select the best mate from the group. Sadly, in an area where there is a very heavy buck harvest annually, the only "breeding" buck in the area could be a yearling whose fitness has not been sufficiently tested by nature.

Once a doe comes into estrus, she becomes agitated and will not tolerate the company of other females. She travels more widely and increases her activity in general. Recent studies on the use of signposts suggest that does visit them, and perhaps even deposit chemicals on them, by rubbing the vaginal area on the tree. It is generally believed by researchers that does can determine at least the social position and physical condition of the buck(s) from the scent of signpost secretions. The receptive female tends to center her activity around the signpost until contact with the "chosen" buck is made. Doe activity becomes very limited as estrus approaches.

The social hierarchy of does also determines the order in which they come into estrus. Normally, the "alpha" and "beta" does within a group will come into estrus earlier than will others, due to the fact that they have staked out the best forage and are thus in better physical condition. In years with good overall forage quality, however, does of lower social standing also might breed early. There is some tendency for the various does within a group to be synchronized, even though not all within the group will come into estrus at once. This could explain why a particular doe group might be the focus of intense buck activity for a short time, then draw little attention until the next estrus cycle 25 or more days later.

Many biologists persist in telling the public that deer die within a mile of where they were born; yet, research over the last decade clearly has showed that this is not always the case. Various studies have concluded that home-range size is determined by many factors and varies widely from one geographic area to the next. In the Pineywoods of Texas, for example, the average home range of does might include only a few hundred acres, while in Mississippi it could exceed 1,000. And for bucks the home range can be huge, frequently exceeding *eight* square miles!

In general, lifetime home ranges for southern deer are smaller than those for northern populations. Home range

When Randy Bean's wife, Donna Lee, found a big set of sheds near their Manitoba home in February, 1992, Randy decided to hunt the buck the next season. In November, he arrowed the 170-class trophy only a short distance from the sheds had been picked up. Not all northern whitetails migrate from their fall range when winter snows arrive.

size is particularly great for whitetails living in areas with heavy snowfall; in such places, they do not behave in a manner much different from that of mule deer. It is not unusual to see a strong migratory pattern in northern whitetails, making patterning much more difficult. In Alberta and Saskatchewan, for example, deer migrate many miles from feeding areas to winter cover when snowfall is heavy. In years with little or no snowpack, this migration might not even occur, whereas in years with extremely high snowfall the animals could move great distances. The farm country provides deer with little protection from deep snow, so whitetails move to the aspen country, where winter browse is abundant and more cover is available. Obviously, in patterning such deer, a good

For several reasons, northern whitetails tend to have larger home ranges than southern deer. Vermont's Richard Duffy shot this huge buck in northern Maine, a region with low deer densities and extremely severe winter weather condtions.

working knowledge of local whitetail behavior is a must, so that you don't end up trying to hunt deer many miles from where they actually spend their time during hunting season!

As noted earlier, whitetail home ranges are elliptical in shape, as seen on a map. Within the home range, there is not equal utilization of every spot; deer favor some areas over others by a wide margin. Home ranges should be thought of as expanding and contracting ellipses, in which whitetails move about from one area of concentration (core area) to another. Again, this is apparently in response to changing foraging conditions and nutritional needs, though hunting pressure also can play a major role.

Home range also changes with age of the animal. In general, yearling bucks tend to have large, unstable home ranges. Once a doe drives off her year-old son during the fawning season, he usually roams in search of other bucks with which to form a social group.

The so-called "dominant floater" is one of the hardest of all bucks to pattern.

However, once a group has been formed, the home range of each buck within it tends to stabilize.

The real exception to this rule is the sort of buck we have come to call the *dominant floater.* For whatever reason, he never settles down into a year-round home range like that of a "normal" buck; he just roams over the landscape, sometimes visiting points a dozen miles or more apart! There is no way to identify this type of buck at other times of year, for during the spring and summer he can have a relatively small, stable home range and associate freely with other bucks. It is only during the pre-rut and rut that he exhibits his unusual travel pattern.

While habitat preferences of whitetails are highly variable, they always are dictated by nutritional demands. Because the primary biological unit of the species is the matriarchal group, deer long ago adopted the previously discussed strategy, in which the females take the best habitat and the males get the rest. This explains why you are most likely to find bucks in low-quality habitats (from a nutritional standpoint) for most of the year.

Although does have well-defined bedding areas, the *sanctuaries* are unique to bucks, which instinctively seek them out. Because the sanctuary is such an important place in the life of the buck, we obviously must be able to identify such places if we are to pattern him successfully. This process will be covered in great detail in Chapter 7, but for now, let's just say that *the sanctuary is the most protected area within a buck's home range.* It provides him protection from intruders, offering him the ability to detect danger early and then to escape via some secure route. A sanctuary could be located deep in a swamp or within a small conifer thicket close enough to a highway for the buck to lie there and watch cars pass. Bucks often have seasonal sanctuaries, to which they return at the same times each year unless significantly disturbed.

Bucks move from their sanctuaries to feeding and staging areas via *travel corridors.* Because matriarchal groups are associated with drainages, bucks' travel corridors also tend to follow these topographic features. In other cases, however, they follow logical terrain and habitat features, including ridge slopes, saddles between drainages and strips of cover in open areas.

While many of the topics touched upon in this chapter might seem totally unrelated, when you put them all together, a clear picture of the whitetail's fascinating lifestyle begins to emerge. Whitetail biology as we know it today is the result of many thousands of generations of deer having come and gone, each adapting in some minor way to the world in which it lived. Over the eons, the species has developed a "society" in which female-oriented family groups dominate the prime feeding areas along the waterways, for purposes of ensuring maximum fawn survival. The bucks have given way to them, moving to relatively poor habitats but staying close enough to the does that

Sanctuaries are special places within a buck's home range. They provide him with great security, offering multiple escape routes in times of danger.

they can be accessed during the breeding season. By visiting numerous matriarchal units during the rut, the various bucks in an area are able to maintain genetic diversity in the herd, contributing to its vitality. This grand script is played out annually, wherever whitetails are found, in a manner that is quite predictable to those who truly understand deer.

Mike Moody's 210 2/8-point monster, Iowa's best buck by muzzleloader, was shot as he made his way from a sanctuary to a feeding area during a winter storm in 1990.

Patterning whitetails within this broad framework of behavior is a process whose procedure varies, though, depending on when during the year you actually begin. In later chapters, we will outline strategies for every time of year, so that no matter when you start or where you hunt, you will be able to lock onto the pattern quickly and effectively. In our next chapter we will discuss how you go about getting the lowdown on your deer herd *before* you leave the comfort of your home.

CHAPTER 3

Getting the Picture

Unfortunately, the average deer hunter has little understanding of his hunting territory. Ask him to draw a map of the place and you come up with some pretty distorted views of geography! We have known folks who owned the same property for 30 years yet never visited some of their best deer country.

Taking a bird's-eye view of your hunting area will open up a whole new world, allowing you quickly to develop an understanding not only of what deer are doing in your area, but also helping you develop an effective hunting plan. But, where do you obtain aerial photographs and topographic maps? Fortunately, the materials are easy to acquire and simple to use.

MAPS AND PHOTOGRAPHS

It is impossible to have too much information about your hunting area. But even if you obtain no other types of information about it, you should acquire as many types of maps and photos as is practically possible. Although the process might seem confusing at first, there is no magic involved in acquiring and interpreting these aids. Basically, you will need both topographic maps and aerial photos.

Dave Engel shot this 250-pound New York buck on a vegetational edge in the woods. This type of structural feature shows up well on an aerial photo.

Topographic Maps

The U.S. government agency charged with producing
and supplying topographic maps and documents is the
U.S. Geological Survey (USGS), headquartered in Reston,
Virginia. The National Cartographic Information Center
(NCIC) makes available maps and photos for most of the
federal agencies, including USGS, Bureau of Land Management (BLM), NASA and U.S. Army, Navy and Air Force.
The USGS is divided into four regions in which whitetails
reside, and maps for each are supplied by a regional
service center:

Region 5 (Eastern Mapping Center)
U.S. Geological Survey
536 National Center
Reston, VA 22092

Region 4 (Mid-Continent Mapping Center)
National Cartographic Information Center
1400 Independence Road
Rolla, MO 65401

Region 3 (Rocky Mountain Mapping Center)
National Cartographic Information Center
U.S. Geological Survey
Box 25046, Stop 504
Denver Federal Center
Denver, CO 80225

Region 2 (Western Mapping Center)
National Cartographic Information Center
U.S. Geological Survey
345 Middlefield Road
Menlo Park, CA 94025

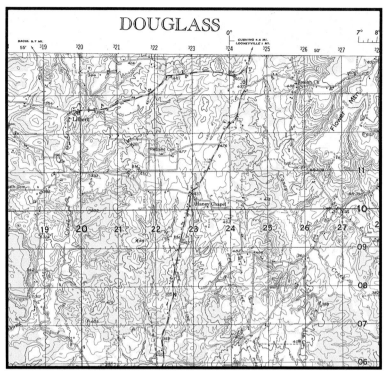

Topographic maps are available from the U.S. Geological Survey (USGS) and follow two formats: 7.5-minute and 15-minute. The large-format 7.5-minute maps are preferable, but may not be available for your area. Here is a typical topo map for an area in Texas. Maps are specifically named quadrangles: This one is the Douglass Quadrangle. The contour interval is 20 feet (see legend inset). Map features such as roads (improved or non-improved), houses, wetlands and streams, and vegetation (green areas) are clearly shown. Refer to the legend for an explanation of map symbols.

In Greek, the word "topographic" literally means "to describe a place." Topographic maps are perhaps the easiest to interpret, because they are line drawings made from more sophisticated mapping and imaging sources. There are two basic scales from which to choose: 7.5-minute and 15-minute maps. The term "minute" is one used by geographers to represent standard mapping units. A minute is 1/60 of a degree. A 15-minute map normally has a scale of one map measurement unit to 50,000, meaning each inch on the map represents 50,000 inches on the ground. This figures out to about 1 1/4 inches on the map per mile on the ground. The 7.5-minute map, oddly enough, is referred to as a large-scale map, because each inch on it depicts a smaller area than on the 15-minute map.

If you wish to determine the distance from one map feature to another, just measure the straight-line distance (inches) and divide by the appropriate scale. For example, suppose you measure the distance on a 7.5-minute map, on which the calculated scale is 2 5/8 inches per mile, and you see that where you park your truck is 1 2/8 inches from your stand. (See map, next page.) Dividing 1 2/8 by 2 5/8 gives an estimated straight-line distance of 0.5 mile.

Topographic maps are packed full of information that can help the deer hunter, the most important of which are contour lines. These lines join points of identical elevation above mean sea level, thus indicating the rise and fall of the terrain in a given location. The distance between contour lines depends on not only the lay of the land, but on the scale of the map as well. A 7.5-minute map might have contours at intervals of 5, 10 or 20 feet, while a 15-minute map might have contour lines at intervals of 20, 50 or even more feet. Each map type shows two types of contour lines — light ones for the standard interval and darker ones for intervals of 50 or 100 feet. High points are marked with the exact elevation above mean sea level. Obviously, the 7.5-minute map generally presents greater

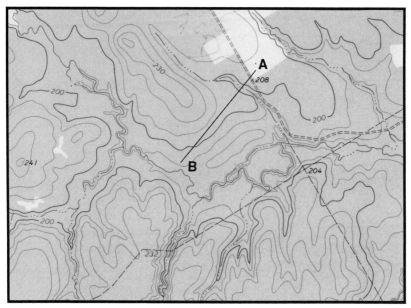

On this topographic map, we have measured the distance between two points (A & B), then calculated the actual distance on the ground. The measured distance between these points is 1 2/8 inches. The scale is 2 5/8 inches per mile; thus, the calculated distance is about half a mile.

detail of the area, so we prefer to use them whenever possible for scouting and patterning whitetails.

Although topographic maps are line drawings, the data used to generate these maps come from many sources, including remote sensing and aerial photos. So, on most topographic maps, you also can determine the general vegetation pattern — at least as it existed when the map was drawn. Wooded and brushy portions are shown in green. Open areas such as pastures and grasslands are left white on the map. Streams, rivers, lakes and wetlands are colored blue and easily identified, using the map legend. (See map, page 31.) Houses, roads, trails and other map features are clearly marked.

As we get further into this chapter, it will become obvious why it is important to have a working knowledge of topographic maps for patterning deer. Probably the singlemost important feature to locate, when trying to pattern deer, is the watershed, or drainage. As discussed in Chapter 2, whitetails are drainage animals, with social groups intimately tied to these topographic features. Bucks follow these while traveling to and from sanctuaries, bedding and feeding areas, as well as when moving toward staging areas. Therefore, you should learn to recognize drainages, saddles and funneling features. Let's look at an example of each.

This 7.5-minute map below clearly shows a complete drainage. The upper limit of the drainage (Spring Branch) is defined by the contour marked *300* (arrow), meaning it is located 300 feet above mean sea level. Each of the lighter contour lines represents a decrease in elevation of 10 feet on this map. The small creek (blue line) located at the

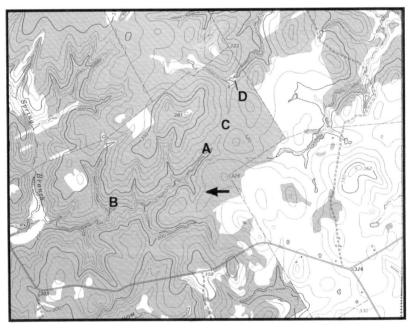

Understanding how to read a topographic map will open up new worlds to the deer hunter. A variety of habitat features easily can be identified using these important reference materials. (See text above for discussion of this map.)

bottom of the drainage cuts across contours. Each time the stream crosses a contour line, we know it is dropping 10 feet in elevation from where it crossed the previous line. From point A to point B, a distance of approximately one mile, the stream bed drops 40 feet, meaning it is following a relatively gentle slope.

Point C illustrates a saddle, an area used by deer when moving from one drainage to the next. Notice the saddle is characterized by having higher elevations to the west and east, with a relatively flat traverse from one drainage to the next. In fact, while actually scouting this area, we found a long-established rub line across the flat ground between the two drainages. The buck(s) apparently were bedding on the upper end of the small point, at D.

Topographic features which force deer to move along a certain contour are called *funnels*. A funnel can be caused by topography and/or habitat. For example, in this map,

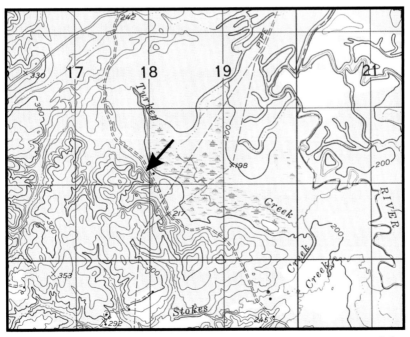

A steep ridge (arrow) adjacent to the swamp created by Turkey Creek creates a funneling effect on deer movement.

the swamp created by Turkey Creek, when combined with the steep slopes to the southwest, encourages deer to travel the drier ground along the 200-foot contour. In fact, one of the largest bucks ever taken from Cherokee County, Texas came from this area. (See photos, pages 45 & 163.)

Other features of interest to the hunter include dwellings, highways and roads of various types. Such features give you a good indication of the extent of access to and use of an area. Because some of the commonly used topographic maps are based on data that now are 40 or more years old, it might be a good idea to update your maps, using county road maps produced periodically by state land-grant universities and natural-resource agencies.

Aerial Photographs

Topographic maps, although very useful, provide just part of the total picture needed for patterning whitetails. A

Black-and-white aerial photos are inexpensive and allow you to conduct preliminary scouting without leaving home.

While color aerial photos sometimes lack the contrast of B&W photos, the human eye is more capable of detecting differences in color shades. Thus, many hunters find color shots more useful for patterning.

working knowledge of aerial photos and their use will add yet another layer of information.

There are two basic types of aerial photos: black-and-white and color. Black-and-white photos usually are inexpensive and for analyzing your hunting territory, sometimes offer flexibility not afforded by color, because they provide more contrast than color photos. Most black-and-whites are shot with what is called "panchromatic" film, meaning all colors are recorded as a continuous gray scale, ranging from solid black on one end to pure white on the other. Although black-and-white films which record only infrared wave lengths of light (just beyond the red end of the visible spectrum) are now available, we have found their utility limited for patterning deer.

There are many sources of aerial photos, including the USGS, U.S. Department of Agriculture (USDA) and state forestry and natural-resources agencies. In most cases, we utilize either the USGS or the USDA Soil Conservation Service (SCS) in acquiring black-and-white photos.

For patterning, perhaps the greatest potential offered by black-and-white photos is stereoscopic application. While this might sound complex, it really is not. Stereoscopes work on a simple principle, an example of which is as close as your own fingers.

Hold your hands in front of your face, with your index fingers pointing at each other. Bring the tips of these fingers toward each other, with your eyes relaxed, until an image resembling a small "sausage" appears, floating between your fingertips. What has happened? Your eyes and brain have created an image from the two slightly different perspectives (one for each eye).

A pocket stereoscope essentially lets you do the same thing with two photos taken of the same geographic area,

Stereoscopes are used to view two overlapping B&W photos simultaneously. By properly positioning photos beneath the stereoscopes, you obtain a three-dimensional view of your hunting territory. This allows interpretation of the area by showing the relative height of trees and other vegetation, as well as subtle changes in elevation.

but from two slightly different perspectives. When the plane flies over the area during the initial photo session, the photographer shoots a series of overlapping photos of the target. Later, by aligning two adjacent photos just right under the stereoscope, you can see a three-dimensional image of the landscape. As opposed to a simple "flat" photo, this allows you to see very minute differences in terrain characteristics, as well as differences in the height of vegetation, such as trees versus shrubs. As you might imagine, these stereoscopic photos are particularly useful in pinpointing funneling features and vegetational edges preferred by deer.

Stereoscopes now are available in a wide range of types and prices; the least expensive is the pocket stereoscope, which sells for around $25. (For

Jim Horan downed this big Maryland buck while hunting a deep ravine — the type of habitat feature that shows up well on maps and photos.

information on ordering one of these, contact Forestry Suppliers Inc. in Jackson, Mississippi.)

The *orthophotoquad* is a special type of black-and-white aerial photo, one that has a modified image which has been adjusted for the distortion produced by camera tilt, topographic distortion and lens distortion. Normally, as you move from the center of an aerial photo to the edges, the image becomes increasingly distorted; this can create problems when you attempt to map your area or overlay an aerial photo on your topographic map. Orthophotoquads adjust for these distortions, allowing you to make very accurate measurements and overlaying on topo maps. You even can obtain orthophotoquads with topographic lines already superimposed on them. These materials are available through USGS and other sources. However, you might find that they offer more precision than is actually needed for patterning deer.

Color aerial photos offer you the ability to interpret the landscape in ways not possible though the use of black-and-white photos. Most humans can discriminate among about 100 times more color shades than gray shades, so having color in the photo greatly expands our ability to discriminate among features. There are two basic types of color aerial photos. First are the standard color images, produced with normal color films. They are available as either prints or transparencies; we suggest prints as being more practical. Prints can be purchased inexpensively and stored easily in a drawer or file folder.

The usefulness of normal color aerial photos depends on the time of year in which they are taken. We find photos obtained during the fall or winter offer the most interpretable information about our hunting territories. At those times, the leaves of hardwoods either are or in full color or absent, allowing us to discriminate between hardwoods and conifers of various types.

Color photos can be obtained in several ways. First, there are the sources listed at the end of this chapter, principally the USGS. The second means is through simply renting a plane (or getting a friend who has one) to fly you over the area in question. You might be pleasantly surprised to learn that renting a plane for short flight of this nature generally does not exceed $100!

Next, you obviously have to take the photos. A 35mm single-lens reflex camera outfitted with a 135mm lens is best for this work. As for altitude, unless you are hunting (or studying) a very small area, you will get the best photographic coverage in one or two frames from 7,000 to 15,000 feet above the ground. Ask the pilot first to pass over the area at approximately 7,000 feet, to see if you can get all (or most) of your area in the viewfinder. If you cannot, increase your altitude until you can. Be sure to shoot a number of photos on different settings, and be sure you are photographing the right tract!

Perhaps the most useful category of color aerial photography is *color infrared*. It has the advantage of allowing you to discriminate among many objects and conditions not visible on normal color or black-and-white films. However, you will need to invest some time in learning what the different colors in these photos mean. Following this chapter, we have included some examples of infrared aerial photos and their interpretations to clarify our points. In addition, the table on page 43 shows the color infrared versus normal color hues for various ground objects and habitats.

If you have a current aerial photo, it helps you identify potential feeding areas, such as clearcuts. Wayne Cox and his guide, Steve Sheaffer, found this trophy Montana buck in just such a place.

Notice from the table that conifers show up as various shades of pink to red in infrared photography, particularly in the cooler months. Hardwoods, on the other hand, show up in a wide variety of colors, depending on their stage of development and the time of year. Drainages and wetlands, which we already have noted are important areas for deer in all habitat types, appear as blue or greenish-blue.

We have included in the table a selection of ground objects that are important to scouting and patterning whitetails. Study the examples and compare them to the color infrared photos provided or to some from your own area. For objects not covered, do some "ground truthing," which means traveling to the area after looking at a photo to see exactly what is showing up in your photos in a certain way. With a little practice, you should have no trouble interpreting aerial photos, no matter what their type or format, just like a pro.

All this might seem very technical, but its well worth the effort. It will save you a great deal of time and effort, as well as allow you to reduce the amount of time needed to scout a particular property. In the next chapter we will take technology one step farther when we discuss some of the new high-tech developments for studying whitetails — developments that raise many ethical questions.

Typical differences in colors for normal vs. infrared aerial photos:

Ground Object	Normal Color	Infrared Color
Conifers, older pines, cedars, spruce, fir, etc.	Green	Pink, magenta
young pines, cedars, spruce, fir, etc.	Green	Magenta, pink
Hardwoods, foliated	Green	Magenta
fall colors	Yellow, orange	Mauve
defoliated	Gray or brown	Green, blue-green or blue
Brushland	Light green	Dark blue-magenta
Open water	Blue, green	Light blue
Wetlands	Blue, green	Blue, dark blue
Plowed fields	Brown, gray	Pink
Row crops	Green-brown, gray	Pink, magenta
Grasslands	Green, yellow, brown	Pink, magenta
Shadows	Blue, detail	Black, no detail

Modified from Murtha, P. A. 1972. A guide to photo interpretation of forest damage in Canada. Can. For. Serv., Ottawa, Canada.

It is important that you learn to interpret patterning features in infrared aerial photos, including: (A) conifers; (B) hardwoods; (C) brushland; (D)wetlands; (E) orchards; (F) agricultural fields; (G) streams and drainages; and (H) hills and ridges. Photos of this type are widely available to the public at an affordable price, yet few hunters realize just how much information they offer.

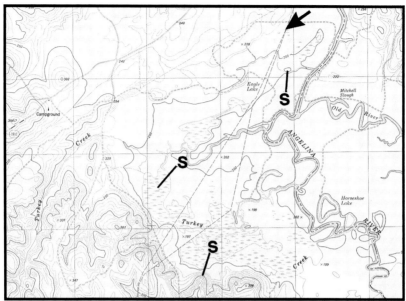

Combining a topographic map and an infrared color aerial photo can give you a powerful tool in patterning whitetails. This example shows where a monster buck (photo, page 163) was taken near Nacogdoches, Texas, along a travel corridor (arrow). Sanctuaries (S) are also indicated on the topographic map; compare their locations to the infrared photo.

How to buy USGS maps[1]

By mail

1. *Using a general catalog of maps (see below), determine which type of map you want to order.*

2. *Write to USGS Map Sales for the appropriate index, price list, and order form for the type of map you want. (See following pages.) See the list of USGS map in dexes. Please note that, for topographic maps, both an index and a catalog are provided for each State.*

3. *When you receive an index, follow the instructions on how to use it, determine the name and identification number of the specific map you want, and fill out the order form (see example).*

4. *If you do not have an order form, write down the name and identification number of the specific map, along with your mailing address.*

5. *Prepare a check or money order made out to "Department of the Interior— USGS." Prepayment is required. For map orders of less than $10, add $1 for mailing.*

6. *Send your order and your pre-payment to:*
   USGS Map Sales
   Box 25286
   Denver, CO 80225

Delivery

The USGS tries to fill mail orders for maps within 3-5 weeks. Various circumstances, however, may prevent prompt filling of an order or part of an order. If the need for your map is pressing, the USGS suggests that you buy over the counter or from a local commercial distributor.

---

[1] *Reprinted with permission.*

Over the Counter

Visit the nearest USGS Earth Science Information Center (ESIC) for answers to your questions, for USGS map indexes, catalogs, and order forms, or for over-the-counter purchase of locally stocked USGS maps. Maps are also sold over the counter at USGS Map Sales in Denver, Building 810, West 6th Ave. and Kipling St., Federal Center, Denver, Colorado, and in Fairbanks, Alaska.

From a commercial distributor

Check your local yellow pages for local commercial outlets that sell USGS maps.

Obtaining assistance

If you need assistance in deciding which type of map you want, getting or using indexes, or identifying and ordering the specific map you want, call or write to one of the ESIC Offices or call 1-800-USA-MAPS. Assistance also can be provided by State ESIC Offices and local map depository libraries.

New maps

Availability of new USGS maps is announced in the monthly list, "New Publications of the U.S. Geological Survey." A free subscription to this list is available from USGS New Publications, 582 National Center, Reston, VA 22092.

Discounts

On an order of maps amounting to $500 or more at the list price, the USGS gives a discount of 50 percent.

Map Indexes and catalogs

Below is a list of USGS map indexes and catalogs and the types of maps covered by each index. They are available by mail *and over the counter from USGS Map Sales in Denver and Fairbanks and over-the-counter map sales ESIC Offices.*

(State) Index to Topographic and other Map Coverage and (State) Catalog of Topographic and other Published Maps (all scales).

> *Topographic maps*
> *Topographic-bathymetric maps*
> *Photoimage maps*
> *Surface-minerals management maps*
> *Ecological inventory maps*
> *Radar image maps*
> *Satellite image maps*
> *Land use maps*
> *U.S., State, and county maps*
> *National atlas maps*
> *Special maps*

Geologic Map Index of (State) (all scales).

> *Geologic maps*

Status and Progress of Topographic Maps (7.5 and 15 minutes).

> *Topographic maps*

Index to Orthophotoquad Mapping

> *Photoimage maps*

Index to a Set of One Hundred Topographic Maps Illustrating Specified Physiographic Features (7.5 and 15 minutes)

  Topographic maps

Index to USGS-DMA 1:50,000-Scale 15-minute Mapping

  Topographic maps

Index to Intermediate-Scale Mapping Index to County Mapping (1:50,000 and 1:1,100,000)

  Topographic maps
  Topographic-bathymetric maps
  Surface-minerals management maps

Index to Land Use and Land Cover Information (1:100,000 and 1:250,000)

  Land use maps

Index to Small-Scale Maps of the United States (1:250,000, 1:1,000,000 and 1:2,000,000)

  Topographic maps
  Topographic-bathymetric maps

CHAPTER 4

Spying on Whitetails

Using aerial photos and topographic maps for patterning deer, as outlined in the previous chapter, is one way of applying technology to the process. But there is an even more advanced level of "high-tech" deer patterning, and that involves the use of sophisticated electronic devices in gathering information about your herd.

For a variety of reasons — including the end of the Cold War — hunters now have at their disposal a dazzling array of "gadgets" that potentially can be applied to the patterning process. Among these are night-vision devices, infrared cameras and even infrared units for detecting warm-blooded targets in low light. "High-tech" definitely has caught up to deer hunting. But with these advancements come not only great opportunities, but also serious responsibilities to utilize them in the proper ways.

The key in determining the ethics of a given piece of equipment or hunting technique lies in being honest with ourselves regarding the application in question. It is quite conceivable that a high-tech device would be used legitimately by one hunter, while another would apply it in such a way as to take unfair (or perhaps even illegal) advantage of wildlife. We are keenly aware of our position in whitetail hunting and management and take that responsibility seriously. We find ourselves dealing with some of these issues on a daily basis, and we do not claim to have all of the answers regarding what is or is not a "proper" use of technology in deer hunting. But given that a variety of technologically advanced products now are on the market and are coming into widespread use, we feel compelled to discuss them.

Bass fishing provides us with a great example of the

A wide variety of high-tech devices are becoming available to the deer hunter, and at prices he can afford. These include (clockwise from upper left): infrared-triggered monitors and cameras; "starlight" night-viewing devices; and infrared units for finding dead/wounded game by body heat.

---

pluses and minuses of applied technology. No other outdoor sport can match it in terms of gadgetry. Some have suggested that bass fishermen don't catch any more fish now than they once did, only that now they know *why* they don't catch any. Seriously, some of the technology now commonly applied to sportfishing actually might serve to enhance the angling experience, by at least making the fisherman more aware of what is going on in the watery environment below him. Understanding such concepts as oxygen depletion, water clarity and temperature-feeding relationships certainly helps in getting the public attuned to such fisheries-management issues as pollution, reservoir construction and land-use impacts. If applied in the proper ways, high-tech hunting devices could have the same positive effect.

We have limited our own use of high-tech devices to those innovations which add to our *enjoyment of studying and hunting the species.* We also limit ourselves as to the timing of their use, recognizing that certain devices, if used during open hunting season, might still be legal to use but not necessarily *ethical.* As a deer hunter, you must set your own standards within the overall framework of what the legal limitations are.

Infrared-triggered cameras let you document the type and quality of bucks present on your land, as well as determine deer activity patterns.

Three of the more intriguing categories of high-tech hunting aids are, as noted, infrared monitors and cameras, night-vision devices, infrared units for locating wounded/dead game, and GPS units. Let's look at each category, to see how they might be applied to both studying and hunting whitetails.

Infrared-triggered Cameras and Monitors

During the 1970s, we became aware of some new devices being used by outdoor-recreation scientists in order to study how humans use recreational facilities. These machines were used primarily for monitoring trail activity; a transmitter emitted a concentrated beam of infrared light, recording an "event" each time a person walked down the trail and stepped in front of the beam. While the exact timing of each event was not recorded, the device did give scientists a count of how many times the beam was interrupted, thus indicating total trail use in a given period. These devices were quite expensive, costing around $600 at the time.

Deer hunters basically remained unaware of this type of technology until around 1980. Up until that time, hunters who wanted to determine trail usage by deer generally would tie strings across the paths, then check to see if/ when they were broken, and in which direction the deer appeared to have been moving. But finally a small California company developed a single device, composed of sending and receiving units, each about the size of a pack of cigarettes. Like the larger units before it, this one recorded the number of times the beam was broken in a given period. But there was an interesting additional development: The unit had a jack for connecting a camera to it. With a camera hooked to the unit, each time the beam was broken, a photo was taken.

Shortly thereafter, the early prototypes of what would become the Trail Master® were developed in Missouri. They were high-tech devices, not only capable of photographing deer, but also recording exactly when the photo was taken. In addition, the number of photos and the interval between them were programmable. Data even could be downloaded from the unit into a computer. Naturally, all of this was quite an achievement, and the Trail Master® opened the door to all sorts of important research projects for whitetail biologists. Other companies began manufacturing similar equipment, including the Trail Monitor® and Camtrac®. As this is being written, some companies are working on incorporating video (both day and night) into their units' capabilities.

Working with Dr. Harry Jacobson of Mississippi State University, James, Ben Koerth and Randy Browning of the Institute for White-tailed Deer Management and Research applied some of this infrared technology to the task of counting deer and studying their behavior. They developed a census technique, using a grid of cameras, which for the first time gave biologists a very accurate estimate of deer populations on a given tract. The researchers also found that accurate estimates of buck:doe and doe:fawn ratios could be obtained in only a few days by setting up such a grid of cameras.

An offshoot of this research occurred on a management area in Louisiana. During the course of the research, the team photographed an extremely large-antlered buck hanging around a particular bait station at night. From the photos, the researchers estimated that the buck was only 3 1/2 years old — but his rack looked to score more than 190 typical Boone and Crockett points! The decision was made to attempt to capture the buck, as he was in a 2,000-acre high-fenced area and legally could be captured alive for use in genetics research. This was the first time a specific buck was photographed with infrared devices and a plan then developed to "shoot" that individual deer.

By utilizing a "starlight" scope, mounted on a tranquilizer gun, the research team was able to dart and capture

These bucks were "captured" using an infrared-triggered camera in Mississippi. Notice that the photograph not only gives you proof of the types of bucks available on your land, but even records the time and date the photo was taken.

that buck the first night an attempt was made to do so. The buck showed up at the same bait station at around his usual 3 a.m. feeding time, and was promptly sedated for transport back to the research headquarters.

Scenarios such as this show the incredible potential for utilizing high-tech devices in a positive way for the purpose of advancing whitetail research. But they also raise some pretty scary questions about what might happen if such equipment were to fall into the hands (legally or otherwise) of a poacher.

Could that buck have been photographed and then shot by an illegal "hunter"? Obviously so. Does that mean we should outlaw the sale and use of infrared cameras by the hunting public? Not at all. Frankly, *every* technological advance, in the wrong hands, could be used for some sort of illegal and/or unethical activity. If these cameras are used solely to gain more information about herd composition and the availability of bucks, and are not used during open hunting season, they would seem to have a place in deer management. Ideally, these devices will be limited to use in the pre-season, in one of the following two ways.

First, there is much to be learned about a deer herd by placing an infrared monitor at a feeding area. (A bait station works best, but is not legal everywhere.) An increasing number of hunters are planting food plots and/or providing year-round food supplements for their deer, in an effort to improve nutrition.

You probably bought this book with the idea that it would help you improve your hunting skills, and it will. But we recommend infrared monitoring devices and cameras primarily because their use can help you get a clearer idea of the overall condition of your deer herd, which is part of the responsibility of being a good hunter. Becoming a deer "manager," as well as a hunter, will involve you more in the day-to-day life of your deer and will help you develop a feel for what the herd is doing. That button buck you photograph next August could turn out to be the trophy buck you harvest five years later. The more you know about your deer, the more respect you will develop for the difficulties they must face each year.

We have found that placing a single infrared camera station at a feeding site or along a trail near the center of a given hunting territory will yield statistically reliable estimates of sex ratios and fawn survival after only a single

This monster Louisiana buck was located using an infrared-triggered camera as part of a research project on deer movements and activity. Using a tranquilizer gun equipped with another high-tech device, a "starlight" scope, research-ers captured the buck in only a single night's effort. Such phenomenal capabilities raise many ethical questions about the use of some types of technology in deer hunting.

week. Ideally, we recommend one camera per 160 acres for best results. Just accumulate photos over a period of 10 to 14 days, add up the number of (different) bucks, does and fawns photographed and then calculate buck:doe and doe:fawn ratios from these numbers. If you do not come up with at least a ratio of 1 buck per 3 does, or .8 fawns per doe, there is something wrong with your herd. More often than not, that "something" is (1) an overharvest of bucks and (2) an underharvest of does. Having too few bucks left in the herd means that competition is diminished, and such tactics as rattling and calling work sporadically, if at all. Having too many does leads to overpopulation problems, which have negative effects not only on the deer herd but on all other local wildlife as well.

The second manner in which monitors and cameras can be used legitimately is in monitoring such buck activities as rubbing and scraping. A well-placed monitor will photograph a buck that, because of nocturnal movement, might otherwise be virtually impossible to get a look at. Early in our research, we learned just how many bucks move only at night, particularly outside of the breeding period of the rut.

Even if you don't have a great deal of money to spend, there are low-tech ways to determine deer movements — techniques that have been used for eons both by primitive and modern hunters. For example, there are inexpensive devices which simply use a single-event timer across a trail to record time of deer movement. Even more simply, we have brushed out trails and even poured water on deer crossings to get good tracks and thus, determine movements. Other hunters have used strings pulled across trails to do the same thing.

The ability to monitor time of use also allows you to establish a movement and activity pattern unique to your deer herd. Although there are environmental cues that influence deer in general, the pattern of deer movement on *your* property will be modified by many factors, including hunting pressure, habitat conditions and sex and age ratios. The information acquired through monitoring deer movement on your land will not only help you develop a hunting plan, but also to make you more aware of the biology of whitetails.

Night-Viewing Devices

One of the most productive ways to pattern deer is simply to sit and watch them. In the past, this largely has been limited to the daylight hours, though in some places it always has been legal to spotlight after dark, provided no weapons are present. Regularly traveling about our hunting areas, viewing deer through binoculars, helps us to accumulate excellent records on specific bucks, including favorite feeding areas, antler development, age, etc.

Night-viewing devices, however, can greatly expand your available viewing time, especially in large feeding areas such as alfalfa or corn fields. They also have the advantage of reducing disturbance; deer do not seem as spooky after dark.

The idea of folks roaming over the landscape at night, flashing unsuspecting deer in the glare of a powerful spotlight, frankly is a bit much, whether legal or not. But the advantage of this, where legal, is that it does show hunters the

Before you buy a night-vision device, make sure it is legal for observing wildlife in your area.

true potential of their area to produce quality bucks — provided, of course, that the bucks have been allowed to reach maturity. The use of night-vision devices is at least a more aesthetically pleasing way in which to check out the trophy potential in a given area.

The fall of the Soviet Union in the early 1990s made available certain types of technology few hunters could previously afford. When we first began studying deer, for example, a "starlight" scope cost more than $10,000. Today, one of these devices can be purchased through the mail for less than $200.

As the name implies, a "starlight" scope uses a highly sophisticated light-magnification system to amplify light emitted by the stars and reflected from the moon. The resulting image, seen through the scope, is greenish in color, but you

Optical devices that allow you to see with only the light of the moon and stars are now available at reasonable prices.

certainly can make out objects in places that appear to the naked eye to be pitch dark. Most of these scopes have low magnification, in the range of 2X or 3X. You thus must get fairly close to deer to observe them undetected, and this requires good "hunting" skills.

Again, before you actually attempt to purchase any night-vision devices, be sure to contact the appropriate wildlife agency, to determine legality. As noted, there is much potential for misuse of this type of technology.

Game Locators

Another type of device that has come onto the deer-hunting scene is the unit which utilizes an infrared sensor to pick up body heat from a wounded or recently killed mammal, for purposes of improving recovery rates of game. These devices have the ability to literally "see" through thick vegetation, aiding the hunter in locating a wounded or dead deer that might be bleeding sporadically, if at all.

Our tests indicate that these devices do have some utility, but not in terms of patterning deer.

One of the concerns wildlife agencies have about such devices is, as you might guess, the potential for misuse by unscrupulous hunters. One game warden informed us that in one test, a person carrying one of these infrared devices was able to locate every rabbit bedded in a weed field. Utilizing high technology in this manner would give the hunter an unfair advantage over his quarry and potentially could devastate certain populations of small game. Even though rabbit hunters might never exceed their daily limits of cottontails, their average bag certainly would increase, causing serious implications for game management.

Potentially, such devices could be used to find deer in thick cover in much the same manner, aiding hunters in setting up ambushes or effective drives. So, it is an area of concern for wildlife professionals in some areas.

Not all high-tech devices are designed to use in patterning. A good example is the infrared sensing device used for locating dead/wounded game.

Global Positioning Systems

There is one last bit of technology that, while it does not really allow us to spy on whitetails, does allow us to accurately determine where we find deer sign and see deer. These are the Global Positioning Systems, known more commonly as GPS. This new technology gained public notice during the Gulf War, when we all were amazed by the pinpoint accuracy of modern warfare.

GPS equipment recently became declassified and was made available to the general public. When we first became aware of these systems, the cost was incredible! In fact, the Institute purchased some of the first equipment for use in deer research for several thousand dollars! Today, the average guy can buy a scaled-down version for a few hundred dollars from al-most any outdoor equip-ment catalog.

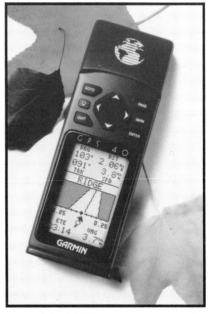

The GPS systems func-tion by communicating with two or more satel-lites. A built-in computer then calculates the unit's location on the earth's surface, using some pretty sophisticated geometry-trigonometry programs. Accuracy is limited by the U.S. Defense Department. Obviously, they reserve the more accurate systems for defense use, but you can expect accuracy to within 50 or 100 feet. They also allow you to record paths taken by yourself or a deer.

Hand-held GPS units give the deer hunter an unprecedented ability to determine exactly where in the woods deer or their sign have been located.

All of the high-tech devices outlined in this chapter have some potential for use by the deer hunter, but not all serve a real purpose in the patterning process. All of them are merely aids, and even the best of them should not be viewed as a substitute for woods skills or time spent in the field. We can pattern deer without using any of these gadgets.

The infrared-triggered monitors and cameras have perhaps the greatest usefulness, particularly in the area of management. They certainly allow landowners and hunters to determine the number and quality of animals in an area more quickly than by traditional methods, and often more accurately.

Night-viewing scopes expand opportunities for viewing deer, especially bucks, in areas with heavy hunting pressure. However, unless they are used in an illegal manner, we can find no advantage they would offer in actual hunting, especially for nocturnal bucks. The exception would be in areas where human drives or running deer with dogs are traditional, accepted hunting practices. Even in such cases, we have serious reservations about the ethics of using these devices.

In short, if you use night-viewing technology to enjoy watching wildlife or to verify existence of a deer you haven't been able to see in daylight, we feel its use probably is acceptable.

Devices designed to help hunters locate wounded or dead deer more efficiently and reliably definitely could be of great use in the right situations, as they could reduce the loss of game. Again, however, they would seem to be of limited use in helping the hunter to pattern deer for hunting purposes.

CHAPTER 5

Your Scouting Plan

Many whitetail hunters think scouting is merely hunting without a weapon in hand. They make a trip or two each year (usually, the weekend before opening day) and wander about the landscape, looking for a deer or at least some sign of a deer's passage. All too often they head home without having found anything noteworthy, but based on what they've seen, have come up with a "plan" for deer season. They saw a buck cross a logging road, or they found a half-hearted scrape or handful of rubs, or maybe they just went back to their permanent stand and nailed up a couple of new boards. And back home that Sunday night, they call up their hunting buddies and announce they've figured out the best place to bag a buck. The fact that so many deer are shot every season is far more a result of large herds than of stellar preparation on the part of hunters.

Patterning requires *serious* scouting, not just a single stroll through the woods around your favorite stand site. Yes, as you hunt a place year after year, you become more efficient at scouting it, and the process requires progressively less time. But at some point you must get out and scout the place properly. Otherwise, you will continue to remain at a distinct disadvantage, and you never will have the kind of success you otherwise could.

But we don't merely want to rush into the woods and start scurrying about, trying to take in everything at once. That usually does nothing more than overwhelm the hunter, and bad decisions often are the result. A mature whitetail buck is a formidable challenge, a sly animal with a sizable home range (in most cases) and a great knowledge of many parts of that range. Thus, when the time comes to tackle the challenge, your first step should be to come up

In early October 1993, Illinois bowhunter Dennis Boaz lived out every bowhunter's dream, taking a massive buck during the first week of archery season. This was a perfect example of the rewards of serious scouting, for Dennis had tracked the buck closely for several months after the previous year's sheds were found nearby. All told, Dennis saw the Boone and Crockett buck 33 times between early July and October. He carefully located the feeding, staging and bedding areas used by the 6 1/2-year-old buck, then developed a winning strategy for shooting the deer on the first day he actually hunted him. The trophy field-dressed a whopping 227 pounds and has 26 scorable points!

with a plan. Your strategy for scouting, as well as hunting, should be determined before you ever set foot in the field.

Again, time (or to be more accurate, the lack thereof) is one of the modern deer hunter's worst problems. It is both inefficient and ineffective to scout in a haphazard fashion, with no real idea of what you're looking for or what it will mean, even if you find it. In scouting, as in actual hunting, you need to get the maximum good out of your time without negatively affecting the natural patterns of your deer.

Quickness is more often the foe of the trophy hunter than his friend. Rushing leads to mistakes, and mistakes lead to failure against any animal as sharp as a mature buck. Even so, we recommend scouting at a fairly rapid pace, particularly if the main purpose of a specific trip is to find and analyze deer sign, rather than merely observe the animals themselves.

This is not to say you should scout superficially, only that you know what you're looking for and then

Experienced deer scouts cover a lot of ground in a short amount of time, because they know where to look for sign and what it means when they find it. Nothing is haphazard.

have the common sense to know what it all means when you find it. With experience, you learn to scout at a lively clip; you go straight to the most likely areas to find the right deer sign, verify its existence and appraise its status and then move along. In the field, it usually is only when you are pondering the exact location of your setups (discussed in detail in Chapter 10) that you stay in an area for very long at a time.

Because we, the authors, are fortunate to hunt some new deer country every year, and because we also hunt in a number of widely separated regions of North America on an annual basis, we have had little choice but to learn how to do this. Perhaps that description applies to you as well; perhaps it doesn't. Either way, you will find that once the principles of this system are known and understood, they will work for you all over the continent, from the brushy plains of northeastern Mexico to the beaver swamps of central Canada and everywhere in between. A whitetail is a whitetail, no matter where he lives!

Why Scouting Isn't Hunting

While it is true that you can (and in many cases, should) scout as you actually hunt deer, scouting in its purest form is somewhat different from hunting. When you're hunting deer, as you move through the woods you primarily are looking for the animals themselves, while keeping an eye out for various forms of sign that might tip you off to the presence of your quarry (e.g., fresh tracks). Your primary purpose is unquestionably to spot and shoot your target animal. But just as it is a mistake to spend all of your hunting time looking down at the ground in front of you, it is a serious mistake to spend all of your scouting time looking for deer. The patterning process obviously includes deer sightings in many cases, but if we had to choose between finding deer visually or simply finding their sign, we would almost always opt for the latter. Good deer sign actually can show you details of a deer's life that could not be equaled by anything less than around-the-clock observation of the animal itself.

Deer sign, in all its various forms, is there for us to see anywhere the animals are found. In some habitats it is much easier to find than in others, but it's there nonetheless. And thankfully, it can be located quite efficiently if we know how to use our reference materials — especially our topographic maps and aerial photos. With those in hand, we can target likely places without ever leaving home, so that when we do get our chance to be afield, we can shorten our necessary scouting time greatly.

Scheduling Scouting Trips

It has been our experience that it takes roughly seven hunter-days to scout a square mile (640 acres) of habitat thoroughly. If you have a partner along, it obviously should take only half that long. Fortunately, you need not burn a week of vacation time on scouting. It can be done a day here, an hour there, so that over a period of months you acquire considerable knowledge of your hunting area and the deer living in it.

If you take advantage of scouting opportunities as they are presented, you will be surprised how much time actually can be spent in the woods each year. Those hunters who enjoy scouting make it a priority, and as a result, get into the woods often. A good example is Bret Giuliani of Dickerson, Maryland, a man who thinks about trophy bucks all year long. "I have 14 bow kills mounted in my home," Bret told Gordon recently, "and guys are always telling me how lucky I am to have shot that many good deer. But they aren't in the woods all the time the way I am. When I'm going someplace and drive past what looks like an interesting piece of woods, if I have even a few minutes to spare and the land is open for hunting, I'll stop and walk around as long as I can. You'd be surprised how much scouting you can get in during the course of a full year if you do that."

Bret is a successful hunter largely because he scouts a lot, and he scouts a lot because he enjoys it. We all make time and money available for those things we most like to do, whether we admit it or not, and hunters who want to scout a lot manage to do so, despite the fact that many other activities and obligations compete for their free time. Those who scout often also find it easier to keep their woods skills intact from one deer season to the next, without that awkwardness most other hunters feel and display every opening day. Yes, it pays to spend time in the woods, even without a weapon in hand!

This wide 11-pointer, shot by Bret Giuliani on October 7, 1991, is one of the top bucks ever arrowed in Maryland. Bret scouts year-round, and his consistent results show it.

If you have a favorite hunting area that lies far enough from home to preclude your "dropping in" whenever the mood strikes you, you probably will benefit from actually making *appointments* to scout it. You even can use a standard appointment-type calendar for keeping track of when you will be scouting. One of the reasons this is a good idea is that you should take a scouting appointment just as seriously as you would a business appointment, and having a written schedule helps you remember it. Then too, if you are hunting land owned by someone else, it is helpful to coordinate your visits with the landowner's own schedule, to ensure there are no conflicts. (Don't assume you can just drop in whenever you like; there might be a family reunion going on down by the creek!)

We obviously do not know, as we write this, exactly when you will be starting the scouting process. Some of you might head into the field tomorrow, others eight months from now. No matter. While some times certainly are far better than others for achieving maximum results from scouting, there really is no *bad* time to be learning about your deer herd. The time of year dictates what you will be looking for and how you will approach each trip, but we never would discourage anyone from getting involved in the process whenever there is a chance to do so.

From the standpoint of patterning buck activity, scouting right after deer season ends makes the most sense. If you are strapped for time in the field outside of open season, and you really want to make the most of your hunting time next fall, concentrate your scouting from late December through the end of the dormant period for vegetation in the area. If we had to narrow down the period even more, we'd suggest starting in mid-January and ending sometime in April across much of the continent. The peak time would be shorter in areas with a long growing season, such as the Gulf Coast region, where ideal post-season scouting conditions might end in February some years. For our scouting efforts to be most productive at this time of year, we want dormant vegetation, because we will be scouting at a fairly rapid pace and want to be able to see as far as possible through the woods. This lets us survey the lay of the land, and the deer sign on it, with maximum efficiency.

Of course, one of the great advantages of scouting in the post-season period is that all of the evidence of the previous fall's rut is laid out for us to see and analyze. Rubs are still reasonably fresh; some, in fact, might show evidence of continued use after the rut. Same for scrapes, particularly in regions with little or no snowpack. The lack of leaves on deciduous plants makes all patterns more obvious. And, not to be overlooked is the fact that we can inspect potential stand sites (including individual trees) and get a realistic view of what they look like just after leaf fall in autumn. This helps us pick spots with adequate visibility of approaching deer but without undue risk of being detected by those animals. And finally, the sooner you scout after hunting season, the easier it is to see evidence of where others have hunted: a candy wrapper or pop bottle or fresh marks on a tree, showing where a climbing stand recently was used. That can give us real insight into pressure patterns.

The period that follows, from early spring through early summer, is one of the more difficult times for scouting whitetails, though it still can be done. Field conditions now are radically different from the post-season; you cannot see nearly as well in the woods. Rubs thus are not only harder to see from a distance, they also have had more time to grow dull in color. Scrapes still are visible to the trained eye, but again, you need to be very close to find them. As for the deer themselves, they have begun to settle back into their warm-season pattern, taking advantage of sprouting crops and native vegetation. Year-old bucks, now growing their first true racks, are wandering about almost at random, seeking new living quarters after having been weaned by their fawning mothers. In short, it is a time of transition in the deer world. The hunter who scouts early in the growing season will have one advantage: the opportunity to find fresh feeding sign that can offer clues as to where deer will be in early fall. (We'll talk about scouting this pattern in Chapter 7.)

July and August are interesting times for both white-tails and those who hunt them. Bachelor groups of adult bucks have formed and are about as visible in daytime as they ever are, feeding in relatively open habitats in late afternoons. While these bucks generally have gathered from a fairly wide area, their visibility does give hunters a good opportunity to assess trophy prospects in the area. It is critical to remember, of course, that these mature bucks will not be wandering about in broad daylight much during open hunting season later in the year.

Only a few of the earliest hunting seasons in North America give hunters a chance to take advantage of this daytime movement. One is in portions of South Carolina, where the gun season opens each August 15. Other early openers, as in Manitoba and Quebec's Anticosti Island, also let bowhunters sample their sport during the velvet period. However, for the vast majority of hunters, the period ending with shedding of velvet is one for observation only.

As bucks come out of velvet, they become progressively more reclusive until the sexual urges of the late pre-rut period bring them out into the open again. September and much of October thus are in many ways a difficult period for scouting. Unfortunately, this is exactly when the average sportsman suddenly realizes deer season is about to begin, and he rushes headlong into the woods for a bit of scouting. In effect, he often does about as much harm as good, bumping whitetails from places where they have grown comfortable after months of nobody being in the woods. Pre-season scouting, as practiced by

In the three photos above, Dave Lacy shows why the effort to find a great hunting spot is worthwhile. He shot all of these trophy bucks in the same small area of Montana over a period of several years. Buck hotspots tend to stay that way year after year.

the masses, sometimes helps the deer more than the hunters. Yet it is possible to learn some important things about your herd even during this time.

South Carolina is one of only a few places where bucks can be hunted with a gun during the velvet period. Ken Boulware got this 14-point non-typical there on August 18, 1990, hunting a clearcut.

How about scouting as you hunt? In special situations, such as a last-minute invitation hunt in a new area, you might have no other choice. However, it is best to do your serious scouting outside hunting season, and then limit in-season scouting to what is essentially monitoring of areas previously checked out. You can check on buck activity during periods when the odds of shooting a buck are poor, such as midday during hot, windy weather or perhaps during a driving rainstorm.

Whenever possible, try to time your trips to minimize the chances of disturbing deer in the area. That generally means scouting during times of low deer activity. In general, during the spring and summer it is not a good idea to arrive on site at first light or late in the evening, unless your purpose is to observe deer from afar. Late morning into mid-afternoon would be better for most scouting. In the winter, on the other hand, deer tend to move more during the midday hours, especially if the weather is severe. Under such circumstances, early or late scouting would be better. Again, think before you act.

Obviously, what you're looking for on a given scouting trip depends somewhat on the timing of that trip. Whereas the goal in January might be to look for shed antlers or pinpoint a stand tree for next November's rut, in August you might simply want to get a look at a known buck, to verify he's come through the summer OK. It's all part of an overall scouting and hunting plan.

Mapping Out A Scouting Plan

All whitetails, including trophy bucks, share a common weakness: *habit.* Each deer develops a movement pattern that allows it to acquire food and shelter daily while minimizing contact with danger. Once that pattern has been established, a deer will not change it unless forced to do so. The fact that patterns *do* shift fairly often is due to the changing nature of food and cover sources, as well as the intrusion of man into the whitetail's world.

But just because a deer shifts its activity pattern does not mean it has abandoned an area entirely; it only means that activity now is occurring someplace else within the animal's home range. Sooner or later, the deer most likely will be back. Determining whether that will happen this month or 11 months from now is much of what patterning is all about.

We like to develop a detailed scouting plan before going to the woods. This involves assigning priorities to each likely spot, then scheduling time for an investigation. Again, it usually takes about seven man-days in the field to thoroughly scout a square mile of deer habitat. About one or two days generally will be needed to get an overview of that area, with the remainder of the time being spent "fine-tuning" the scouting report.

Before you ever make that first scouting trip, you should think hard about what your overall plan of attack will be. Where are you going first? How are you going to get there? What do you think the deer are doing at this time? Again, the answers to these questions will vary with the type of habitat you're scouting and the time of year scouting occurs. We must refer back to our knowledge of deer biology to give us some answers about deer patterns, because the species' physiological requirements change with the seasons.

In the winter, deer seek cover above all else, especially in regions hit by heavy snowfall. The animals actually feed little in many cases. Deer in the Great Lakes region, for example, might move into heavy-growth areas of conifers or hardwoods, whatever will give them a break from the severe weather. Cover also can be provided by topography, such as a deep valley or south-facing hillside where the sun offers a bit of extra warmth. Finding such places is easier if you use your topographic maps and aerial photos in combination.

The importance of winter food sources depends on the geographic location and current weather conditions. For example, deer in snow country seldom venture from yarding areas when there is heavy snow cover (higher than the knees on a deer). They instead munch on whatever woody vegetation they can find in the yard, rather than trying to blaze trails to new food sources. Whitetails simply are not well adapted to plunging through heavy snow, and they sustain many injuries while trying to do so. In such a situation, it would make little sense to

It's important to know what deer do during winter in your area. This is especially true in places where deer routinely migrate to wintering grounds. Don't be fooled into thinking post-season sign was made during hunting season.

scout during the winter around many of the fields and other feeding areas frequented by whitetails in the fall.

Likewise, if your scouting begins in late spring or early summer, it makes little sense to examine stands of mature oaks for fresh deer sign. At that time of year, deer will be browsing on native vegetation and agricultural crops; acorns from last fall are long gone, and this year's crop hasn't yet begun to fall. If you are starting your scouting in late summer, deer usually will be concentrated in the few remaining areas with more digestible foods, such as maturing agricultural crops, fruit orchards and native mast (grapes, berries, etc.) that provide energy for the coming rut and winter.

We certainly are not suggesting that you ignore currently unused habitat features, only that you focus initially on what the deer are doing at the time you begin your scouting program. We will discuss later what all of these activities mean. For now, just concentrate on putting together a meaningful field plan.

It's best to plan your trips to examine only one or two features of the land. For example, let's say you decide that next weekend you will be looking at potential cover areas. You can use your maps and photos to develop a plan for systematically visiting all cover features in the hunting area and making notes of what you find. (It's actually a good idea to number various areas of a single type, so you can keep track of them in the future most efficiently.) After you have searched out the cover areas, make plans to search out potential feeding areas and travel corridors. The trick is to be systematic. Whitetails do not move randomly, and neither should you — particularly if time is short.

Identifying Scouting Locations

Hunters who never have used topographic maps or aerial photos for patterning often are surprised to learn how well these materials work for identifying prime deer

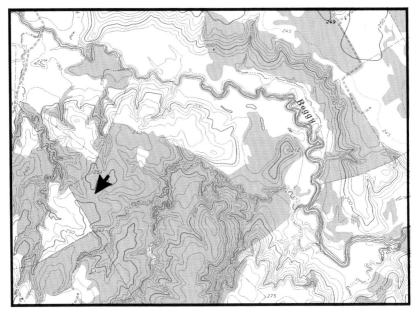

Topographic maps allow you to home in on specific high-probability areas, such as this saddle (arrow) connecting two drainages. Stream channels are indicated by solid or broken blue lines, and vegetated areas are colored green.

areas. You still must investigate each site, but a lot of scouting time can be saved by knowing what a good spot looks like from an overhead view.

Let's start with what we know deer need in their daily lives: cover, food and water. We do not need to find all three features in one small area, though that sometimes is the case (particularly in the southern U.S.). What we really want to find is prime cover areas that give the deer secure access to food sources and, to a lesser degree, water. The actual distance of separation among these components is not as critical as many hunters think, because whitetails habitually cover more ground in a day's time than they are often credited for. (Forget that old notion about deer living their entire lives within a square mile; it seldom is the case.)

The first thing to do is locate all drainages (usually blue

lines on your topo map). Drainages are of the utmost importance to deer because they feature a lot of what the animals need. Water helps plants flourish, so much of the heaviest cover in an area is often found along drainages; and, the soils associated with them are of higher quality. This increases the chances of finding bedding cover and palatable forage there, especially in more arid regions. Obviously, deer are most likely to be able to find drinking water in drainages as well, though much of their daily need for moisture is satisfied through eating juicy plant material. And finally, because drainages are by definition lower in elevation than are areas surrounding them, deer can travel along these routes with a greater feeling of security in many cases. Travel paths most commonly occur along a

It may be difficult to find travel corridors on the ground, but with an infrared aerial photo, it is a simple matter to locate features that funnel deer movement. In this photo, notice it is completely logical to assume deer travel across the cutover area using the streamside management zone (arrow), an area left uncut to protect against erosion. The next step is to go to the area and check it out for deer sign.

When starting your search for doe groups, begin with the most obvious feeding area, such as this alfalfa field. Then, find the closest areas (arrows) providing bedding cover.

---

contour line, midway between the ridge and stream channel. All of this adds up to making drainages — big or small — prime places to start our search for whitetails. Highlight or mark them in some way on your map.

Because drainages represent some of the best deer habitat, it makes sense they are dominated for most of the year by doe family groups, as discussed in Chapter 2. Mature bucks yield these prime spots to the does for almost the entire year, the lone exception being during the breeding period, when the males come to the females. So, it is quite possible to locate rutting sign within doe areas, even though the buck making that sign might "live" a mile or more away during other times of the year. Identifying the home ranges of doe family groups is our first step in getting on the area's overall pattern of whitetail movement. Where the does are will influence the location of bucks, no matter the time of year. The bucks either are giving ground to

One of the many advantages to using color infrared photos is that it allows you to quickly locate and distinguish between habitat features. In this photo, the drainage is clearly marked by the signature color (bluish-gray) of hardwood vegetation in the lowlands, as opposed to the pinkish color signature of the adjacent upland conifer stands.

them, moving to lower-quality areas, or are associated with them for breeding purposes. Either way, does have a profound effect on where bucks are at any point in time.

Does generally do not travel far between bedding and feeding sites unless they have no choice but to do so. Thus, it is quite easy to identify prime feeding areas, then simply look for the nearest available security cover, in order to locate doe bedding areas. Sometimes these will be only a few hundred yards apart, as in the case of does and fawns bedding in a briar thicket and traveling to a nearby soybean field to feed. In the case of a southern clearcut that's three or four years old, the bedding and feeding spots even can be one and the same, which makes patterning seem a bit more of a challenge. But, it's really easier with southern deer, because once you have located does, you know they are spending most of their time in that specific location. You do not have to search out bedding areas. By contrast, in areas where big-woods habitats butt up against scattered fields, does and fawns could be trekking several miles between bedding and feeding. Low deer densities in such areas also contribute to the fact that the animals have expanded home ranges.

Given this, the next step in locating likely scouting locations is to examine your aerial photo. Locate on the photo the drainages highlighted on your topographic map. This might take some practice, because you have to learn the "signature" colors or pattern of streamside vegetation. Mark these same streams on your photo in some way; then, look for thick cover adjacent to them. Also, look for agricultural fields, stands of oaks and other potential feeding areas. Mark these as well.

We fully realize that it is one thing to identify likely places on a map or aerial photo, only to go into the field and find no evidence of the deer activity you expected to see there. Not every suspected bedding area will turn out to be one, but with practice, you should hit on a high percentage of your predictions. Remember: Reference materials are a starting point to save you time on the front end of the process, as well as to give you a documented record of what you find in the woods. Don't be discouraged if your first predictions of where the deer are turn out to be a little off base; stay at it, refining your knowledge as you go.

What about cover areas favored by bucks? Can we use our maps and photos to zero in on them as well? Yes! However, by their nature mature bucks are somewhat solitary animals in most cases, so they often utilize bedding spots slightly different from those used by groups of does and fawns. The first thing to remember is that bucks usually have larger home ranges than do does, and they commonly travel farther between bedding and feeding locations. This means prime buck bedding areas can be smaller and farther off the beaten path than are those favored by female deer, though this is certainly not a hard-and-fast rule.

We will be talking about the most significant type of buck bedding areas — sanctuaries — in Chapter 7. For now, simply understand that these are the most special part of a buck's home range, because they are his protection against danger. Once you have located a big buck's favorite hideout, it is knowledge to be treasured, for it is one of the keys to hunting him successfully.

One of the most important features for patterning whitetails, other than the drainage, is the *saddle*. (See map on page 76.) A saddle is a topographic feature, representing a lower area, occurring between two drainages, which connects them. Because saddles provide an easy, safe way for bucks to move from one drainage to the next, they make excellent stand (setup) locations. Once such spots have been located, using your topographic map, examine your aerial photo to confirm that the vegetation in the saddle permits daytime buck movement. For example, an open field situated right in the saddle certainly could curtail buck travel during legal hunting hours.

Hopefully, by now you can see that if you use your topographic maps and aerial photos in the right way, you can save yourself a tremendous amount of time that otherwise would be spent wandering about the terrain without purpose. It's much easier to find a few spare minutes at home to look over your maps and photos and plan out a scouting trip than it is to drive to your hunting area and do all of the work with your feet. Again, you can't scout a place strictly on the basis of maps and aerial photos, but you *can* cut out a lot of the hours that otherwise would be wasted fighting your way through barren woods. This lets you save your field time for studying the areas really being used by deer and coming up with strategies for hunting them successfully.

Scouting Equipment

There is nothing worse than going afield without the right gear, and it's as true when scouting as when actually hunting. Now that you are making plans to conduct you first visits to the hunting area, it is time to think about what you will be taking along to help you accomplish your goals.

Missouri's Ben Gibson says he scouts "365 days a year." A lot of his time is spent checking out new areas, so he'll be able to react quickly when local deer patterns change.

In many cases, you will be in the woods when conditions are far different from those encountered during open season. It could be 30 degrees below 0 or 100 above. So, one of the first concerns is dressing properly. Remember that you likely will be moving much more quickly in scouting than you would if actually hunting, so you can get by with less clothing than you might think. The same considerations apply to your selection of footwear for scouting. Get a good pair of boots, preferably made of material that won't transfer human odor into your hunting area. (While scouting you aren't going to be overly concerned with deer knowing you have been in their range, but it still won't help to advertise the fact more than necessary.)

During some portions of the scouting process, you will need binoculars. We prefer a magnification at least 10X, but even a low-powered pair beats nothing. The glasses will be used primarily for observing deer, but they also can help you scan for rubs during the post-season, etc. Because carrying binoculars all day can be tiresome — even with a

No matter whether you go the high-tech route or use a more basic approach, when scouting you'll definitely need a good notebook for taking field notes, as well as binoculars and your various topographic maps and aerial photos.

neck strap — you might purchase one of those elastic straps that hold glasses securely against your chest. Another option is to carry your binoculars in a light backpack.

Of course, there are other important pieces of gear as well, including a compass (and possibly a GPS unit), your notebook, topographic map, aerial photo(s), pen and colored pencils for marking your maps. For taking notes, we like to use either a small (6x9-inch) spiral notebook or one of those bound record books found in most stationery shops. Depending on how large your maps and photos are, they can be carried either in map tubes or in folders in your pack.

We also like to take along a small 35mm camera for recording significant features found in the field. Most hunters find color prints more useful than slides. You might even find it worthwhile to tote a small video camera, such as one in the 8mm format. Some of these weigh no more than a couple of pounds, yet they can take excellent footage of habitat features, deer sign and even live white-tails you encounter. (By the way, many landowners love to see footage of deer on their property; compiling a homemade video of various clips can do wonders for your relationship with the person whose land you hunt!)

Tom Foss (left) and Terry Raymond patterned this big Alberta buck. Two hunters working together can scout an area in half as much time.

Some hunters like to use ATVs while scouting, but we feel their use leads to poor results in many cases. The problem is not with ATVs, but with those who use them to run helter-skelter through the woods. Hunters tend to spend more time driving vehicles than looking for sign of deer. The problem is even worse if you try to scout from a standard vehicle, such as a pickup truck. Yes, you can cover more territory in the same amount of time; however, you won't see much of what's there. A "windshield cruise" might be OK for the fair-weather deer hunter, but the consistently successful hunter wears out a good bit of boot leather outside hunting season.

In the next chapter, we'll move the scouting process from the kitchen table to the woods. At long last, you get to scout in a physical sense — but unlike most of the other hunters you know, you're a step ahead.

Chapter 6

Mapping Rubs & Scrapes

Many members of the deer-hunting public go about the woods with clouded minds. They see no patterns of whitetail movement, only homogenous habitat in which deer appear to wander aimlessly. If you often find yourself a victim of that mindset, we have good news for you: Over the next few pages, we will begin to blow away the clouds, showing you that everything a whitetail does is in fact quite logical.

You need to understand only two primary concepts in order to pattern whitetails. First, you need to find something — a scrape, a rub, maybe a buck feeding in an alfalfa field. Exactly what it is really doesn't matter at this point. Second, you need to realize that *regardless of what you have found, it is connected to everything else.* Deer sign and sightings are not isolated observations; they're interconnected events which, when viewed as part of the "big picture," help tell an easily understood story. Read on, and watch the clouds begin to fade away.

Finding and Interpreting Rubs

In patterning whitetails, we are always searching for keys that will open some door on a buck's life and improve our chances of harvesting him. We marvel at the tracking abilities of subsistence hunters and even our own forefathers, but many of us fail to realize that the capacity to revive such skills still lies within us, waiting for a chance to be developed again.

Chapter 2, as you will recall, dealt in part with the biology of chemical and visual communication strategies of deer. Remember, rubs and scrapes serve various purposes, but foremost among these is communication. Let's look at rubs first, to see what they can tell us about our deer and how to hunt them.

Virtually all hunters know that rubs are trees, shrubs and vines (and sometimes even fence posts and utility poles!) on which bucks have rubbed their antlers. But there are many types of rubs, and each tells you something about the buck(s) that made it. The ideal time to find and analyze rubs is right after deer season, but it can be done any time, provided you have an eye trained to the task.

The true student of rubs knows the same places often are rubbed year after year. This is because, barring major changes in the habitat, buck patterns themselves seldom change radically from one year to the next. While rubs occur throughout a buck's home range, certain places within that range

Learning to determine the relative age of rubs allows you to make decisions about the maturity of the buck(s) making them, as well as the approximate length of time since they were made. Most hunters can correctly identify freshly constructed rubs (above), but it takes experience to recognize old rubs. The rub at right was made two years earlier, and damage to the wood has healed over.

are favored far more than others for rubbing. Because the act of rubbing is carried out largely in proportion to the time a hard-antlered buck spends in a given area each year, finding and interpreting rubs is a fundamental part of developing a hunting plan for most mature bucks. Even if the buck rubbing on a line of trees this fall dies or for some reason relocates before next season, chances are good that another buck will move in and rub on his original trees. Old-timers used to call these "buck runs," and in essence they were right. Such places are ancestral in nature and are obviously worth finding.

Getting a feel for buck patterns over time requires you to be able to recognize old rubs. Anybody can spot a fresh, oozing rub with strips of bark hanging off it and yellow inner wood practically glowing in the woods, but to zero in on weathered rubs from the past is a skill many have failed to master. The most easily identified of old rubs are large ones that have healed over. In most parts of North America, serious antler rubbing occurs right at the end of the growing season for trees, just as they are becoming dormant. The buck rips away the bark with his antler bases and beams and then moves along. Were such damage to occur during the growing season, the plant would try to repair it right away; however, if the damage occurs during the dormant season, no such repairs will occur until the following spring. During that next growing season, a heal mark develops on the rub, but it may or may not completely cover the scar.

The next fall, the same buck might well come down the same trail and rub the same tree. (By now, both the deer and the tree have grown larger.) New damage is done to the tree, often right on top of the old scar. The next year, healing occurs again. It is not unusual, in areas with good age structure among the buck population, to find rubs that show heal marks from three or more years of rubbing. Although you have no guarantee that each year's rub was made by the same buck, such repeated use does indicate a larger buck is using the tree — especially if it is of substantial diameter. A rub with three heal marks on it probably represents the work of a buck five or six years old. (We'll talk more about rub size vs. buck size in Chapter 8.)

Many hunters discount the importance of small rubs, as they labor under the misconception that big deer only rub on big trees. The fact is that the biggest buck in the state probably rubs, at least some of the time, on tiny saplings and twigs, as well as hefty tree trunks. It thus pays to learn to recognize old rubs on small trees, which can be a bit trickier than finding the big ones. In many cases, a small tree will die back the year after it has been worked over by a buck. The damage is too severe, and the top of the plant dies. The roots are still vigorous, though, and the tree will sprout from its base. Hence, you should watch for dead stems with several "suckers" protruding from the base.

Young trees that have been rubbed repeatedly often die from accumulated injuries. A telltale sign of such old rubs is the presence of many living sprouts growing from around the base of the dead stem.

It also is important to learn to estimate *when* a rub was made, for that can tip us off to how a buck's travel and activity patterns shift over time. Rubbing exposes the inner wood, and that wood weathers at a noticeably different rate for each species of tree. Some species, including pines, also respond to the damage by secreting copious amounts of pitch. Even this can tell you something about how old the rub is; a rub made before the tree went dormant will have much more sap on it than one made after dormancy set in. The wood of some tree types, including oaks, tends to change color as the rub ages. In order to become more adept at gauging the age of rubs in your area, do a simple experiment: Make rubs on various species of trees, then periodically return and photograph them. You will begin to see that some trees weather quickly, while others look almost as fresh a month later as they did when you gouged them. You can keep these photos in your field notebook and refer to them

Sometimes the age of a rub is obvious. Bits of bark on fresh snow are a sure sign a buck has recently worked the tree.

whenever you want to make an educated guess as to the age of a real rub.

Other clues can be helpful as well, of course. In the weeks before leaf fall, check around rubs for small branches that might have been twisted off by the deer's rack. If any leaves remain on these damaged branches, you sometimes can estimate how long it's been since they started to wilt. (This goes for overhanging limbs on scrapes, too.) Of course, if you know it snowed three days ago but not since, a rub with bark on top of the snow indicates use in the interim. Again, it's all just a matter of applying common sense.

Locating sign with a minimum of effort is where all of that initial "office work" pays off. On your topographic maps and aerial photos, you looked for places you felt would be of use to bucks in their travels during hunting season. As we'll discuss in more detail a bit later, these can be bedding areas, feeding areas, staging areas or the trails linking these features (travel corridors). For a variety of reasons, we tend to favor hunting these corridors over most other portions of a buck's home range, so any time you run across a rub on a deer trail, it is well worth making note of.

Finding a rub is much like coming out of the woods at the edge of a highway: you might be able to see only a small portion of that highway, but you know it runs a great distance to your left and right. Finding a rub essentially means you have found a "deer highway." It might appear isolated from other buck sign, yet it is still part of a much larger picture. In the vast majority of cases, rubs are made by bucks as they travel from one place to another. All you have to do is turn in the proper direction and start following.

Whether you decide to turn right or left should not be an arbitrary choice. You turn in the direction the buck traveled. He is quite willing to share this information, even if there are no tracks to go by, for a buck almost always rubs the side of the tree from which he approaches. In other words, if you are on a north-south deer trail and come upon a tree rubbed on its south side, you can safely assume the deer was traveling north when he stopped to work the tree. If both sides are worked, of course, it implies two-way travel, which hopefully can be substantiated with tracks on the trail. Such rubs are a delight to find while scouting, for these two-way "streets" generally carry more deer traffic than do one-ways.

When you find one of these routes, what do you do first? Stop, pull out your map and/or photo and mark the location as precisely as you can. If you're carrying a GPS unit, use it to record the location even more precisely, but still put it on your reference materials. Some of the more expensive GPS units have a data-recording feature which, when later connected to your personal computer, allows you to draw a precise map of the rub line. But for those

Signposts often are found in staging areas and serve as "billboards" advertising the dominant buck's social status.

---

hunters without the money or inclination to purchase such technology, a simple mark on the map/photo will suffice.

How far does this "highway" extend? That's difficult to say until you check it out. Usually, it will extend much farther than you will be able to follow on your first scouting foray. Subsequent trips to the property will let you find out more about the trail. As the map begins to fill up with rub locations, you might even discover that what you thought were two separate buck trails actually are part of the same one, which can shed welcome light on the overall travel pattern.

Of course, if you are hunting a relatively small property, your rub line trail may very well extend off the area you control. Although this seriously complicates the patterning process, you need to be aware of the realities of modern whitetail hunting. The guy next door may not be as dedicated to the species as you are, and may be shooting everything that walks. Hence, knowing by which paths bucks enter and leave *your* property is even more important in this situation.

Remember that a buck does not rub with uniform frequency as he travels. As was noted in Chapter 2, his testosterone level is highest when he wakes up, meaning he has a lot of pent-up aggressiveness. Rubbing in or near his bedding spot helps to relieve these feelings. He will continue to rub some on his travel corridor leading to a feeding area, whether he is looking for food, does or both. But as he moves farther from his bed, his aggressiveness fades; hence, his rubs become fewer and farther between.

Ever watch a young boy as he arrives at a ball game? At first, he is all smiles as he approaches the field. Upon seeing his playmates, however, he begins to walk more assertively and tries to look as big and mean as he can. It is an instinctive attempt to show dominance over his peers. A buck is much the same way as he approaches a concentration of other deer. He wants to make it clear that he is boss. He suddenly begins to rub more. That's one reason staging areas — places of frequent whitetail interaction — usually contain a lot of rubs.

So, the general shape of a rub line, when viewed on a map or aerial photo, is similar to that of an hourglass — larger at either end than in the middle. In most cases, individual rubs are hit on only one side if the rub is in a travel corridor, while the tree often is hit from several sides (over time) if it is in either a sanctuary (bedding area) or staging area. We will be talking about these areas in greater detail later.

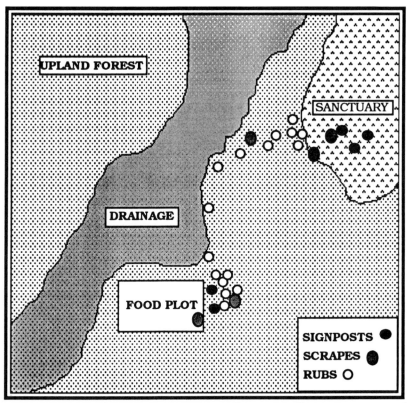

As you map rubs, you start to see that not all areas are used equally. In general, rubs are created in proportion to the amount of time a buck or group of bucks spends in an area.

Once you have a lot of rubs on your map, you can begin to play "connect the dots." Now, a distinct pattern begins to emerge. As you gain experience in looking at your hunting land in this manner, you will see that the rub lines tend to follow the contours of the land and cover and are, as noted, quite logical in their placement. Eventually you reach a level of understanding that allows you to walk through the woods, even without any rubs in sight, and predict where you will pick up the rub line again. Subtle depressions in fallen leaves often are your only clue as to a lightly used (buck) trail during the off-season. You look for this, make a logical decision about where the trail *should* be heading, and pretty soon start finding rubs again. Now, as Sherlock Holmes was fond of saying, "The game's afoot!"

If predicting the locations of deer trails seems impossible to you, rest assured it is only because you haven't practiced it enough. It's something you learn. Sooner or later, you actually begin to think as deer do, and you find yourself walking the same routes they take, even when you're not trying to do so. The same ease of travel that causes you to take a certain line through the woods beckons whitetails to do so, too. As you start to see where bucks rub, you will get a feel for why such patterns have developed, and that gives you greater insight into predicting rub locations in other habitats. The more rub lines you

follow and map, no matter where you hunt, the more you will come to understand how a buck thinks and reacts to his world.

As noted, rubs come in all sizes, from "thrashings" of scrubby brush to full-blown attacks on mature trees and fence posts. Do not fall into the trap of thinking, however, that big bucks rub only on big objects. Mature whitetail bucks, as we noted earlier, will rub on almost any tree or shrub they encounter when in a certain frame of mind. Even the smallest of these can be a signpost, as discussed

Illinois bowhunter Stan Potts relies heavily on the presence of big, fresh rubs to show him where mature bucks travel. This strategy has helped him become one of the nation's most successful hunters of trophy whitetails.

earlier. These special locations are used primarily for scent communication with does and other bucks. When the forehead and lower antler area is rubbed on the signpost, a combination of forehead and tarsal gland scents are placed there for other deer to "read."

Signpost rubs occur primarily in two types of locations. First, every dominant buck has one or more signposts within a few yards of his sanctuary. These rubs are easily recognized by the fact that they have been hit from several sides. This happens because the buck does not always approach the tree from the same direction; a sanctuary is essentially a "hub of a wheel." In addition, the buck's habit of loafing in the sanctuary means he wanders about it, and he frequently takes a few minutes to work on his main rubs. If you draw a line through the intersection of all signposts around a sanctuary, the intersection of these lines almost always is within a few feet of the buck's favorite bedding spot! This can be quite valuable information, because we want to know where the buck feels safe. We will discuss the anatomy and use of sanctuaries more in Chapter 7.

Of just as much importance to the hunter is the location of a second type of signpost rub: the *staging* signpost. These rubs, as you might imagine, are found in staging areas, such as thick cover adjacent to major feeding areas.(See photo on page 91.) Many deer, both bucks and does, encounter the rubs as the animals make their way to food sources.

A third type of rub occurs along the boundaries of the loose "territory" a buck sets up during the rut. (We realize that whitetails are not territorial in the strictest sense.) A buck does not normally venture beyond these markers, so we refer to them as *boundary* rubs. They could be a form of signpost, but as yet, that has not been proved. A good way to identify boundary rubs is to note how they relate to the trail itself. Whereas trail rubs are oriented along the direction of travel, boundary rubs are made *perpendicular* to the trail. Observation of bucks making such rubs indicates that they turn off the travel corridor trail, lean into the rub tree and mark it, both with antlers and forehead. The buck might even mark the overhanging limb with his forehead, antlers and tongue. Finding a boundary rub means you have established the limits of what can be loosely termed the buck's "territory."

Stereotypic buck behaviors are "released" by a variety of stimuli. Scraping and rubbing are classic examples of this phenomenon. Believe it or not, this buck is not even aware of what he is doing!

Mark all rubs on your maps and photos, indicating the type whenever possible. We prefer to use colored pencils to show the various categories: red for signposts, blue for trail rubs and yellow for boundary rubs. Later, we will discuss keeping track of this information using a record-keeping system, and interpreting what it means. You will generate such an enormous volume of information, it is important to be able to handle this material. For now, we simply are scouting and making notes of what we find.

Finding and Interpreting Scrapes

With as much as has been written about scrapes and scrape hunting in recent years, you might figure every deer hunter in North America would understand a great deal about this type of sign. However, a surprising number of hunters, particularly novices, still have a hard time with

Every hunter "knows" scrapes are good places to hunt, but the real trick is knowing which ones produce and which ones don't. Chalmer Adams picked the right ones on November 12, 1989, in Morgan County, Kentucky. This impressive 10-pointer checked his ridgetop scrape line after sunup and offered the young shotgunner a 30-yard shot.

the topic, apparently due in part to the fact that the terminology of whitetail hunting is not the same all over the continent. Some hunters have always called antler rubs "scrapes," because the term seems to describe the action that resulted in the rub; after all, a buck "scraped" his rack against the tree, didn't he?

Of course, the scrapes we're talking about are not rubs, but pawed areas, usually occurring beneath overhanging branches, in which deer urinate. In many cases, a signpost will be nearby; in fact, often it is on the tree whose branch is hanging over the scrape. A fresh scrape is easy to recognize, with the scratched-up earth showing obvious signs of pawing. However, if you also learn to identify old scrapes, just as with old rubs, you will be a step ahead of many other hunters.

Because many scrapes (but not all) are worked repeatedly, they are relatively easy to find, even when covered with leaves and other debris. But the first trick, of course, is to look in the right places. This is an ability that improves with experience, but after a while you can almost predict beneath which branches you are likely to find scrapes. Terrain features and habitat types are the main clues in finding scrapes.

The popular literature are filled with all sorts of classifications of scrapes; some authors have suggested a great number of types exist. Certainly there are different categories, but we doubt more than three. Now, before we get into what they are, let's step back and take a broader view of scraping behavior and why deer exhibit it.

Scraping actually is part of a more complex behavior pattern. It is combined with rub-urination, the stereotypic behavior in which a deer brings its hind legs together beneath its body and urinates down those legs. (Notice that we keep using the word "deer" instead of "buck." That's because, as you might recall from Chapter 2, does also rub-urinate — and they even make scrapes! That's right, does make scrapes, especially in staging areas. But back to the story.)

Animal behaviorists report animals have what are known as *fixed action patterns* (FAPs). These are behaviors which, once evoked, are performed to completion *without the animal really understanding what it is doing.* Even humans exhibit FAPs. For example, consider what happens when a guy is put into an embarrassing situation: He scratches his head. Why? It is a FAP, triggered by embarrassment, and he can't help himself. Scraping in whitetails is much the same. The first cue which can trigger scraping is when a deer meets a deer unfamiliar to it. Both does and bucks will rub-urinate and scrape upon encountering an unknown deer. Presumably, this establishes a scent identity for each deer to remember, and it helps them to establish a pecking order.

Scraping also is released by other cues. Just as the scent of another dog's urine will elicit the stereotypic marking behavior in male dogs, the smell of another buck's scrape or even the visual cue of exposed inner wood on a rub or a pawed-out spot on the ground will prompt scraping behavior. And finally, there is out-and-out, deliberate

Some of the most visited scrapes are in areas with a lot of deer interaction. Billy Bryant's 16-point Tennessee buck was shot as it checked a scrape in an area where Billy had seen 19 does in two days.

signpost scraping and rubbing by dominant bucks, sparked by the presence (or even scent) of does in a staging area. Because some of these locations obviously are more favorable for hunting than others are, when you find a scrape, you need to establish why it was made.

Too many hunters find scrapes and then sit on them for an entire deer season, stubbornly waiting for the return of the bucks that made them. That makes about as much sense as finding where a dog stopped and marked a tree, then waiting for it to return. Maybe it will, maybe it won't. Years ago, outdoor writers loved to say that rubs were places bucks visited only once, while scrapes were places they visited again and again. In reality, the opposite is often true. We definitely should not assume that every scrape will be worked after it has been established. Again, it depends on why the scrape was put there in the first place.

The vast majority of pawings are *trail* scrapes, made

haphazardly by bucks as they travel along their trails. The circumstances eliciting this behavior seldom will be apparent to us, but of more importance is realizing that few such scrapes are used with frequency. Next are *boundary* scrapes, usually found in association with boundary rubs. As with the rubs, these obviously serve to define the outer limits of a buck's "territory." Finally, we have the *signpost* scrape, the function of which already has been discussed. You pretty well can count on the buck that established a signpost scrape returning to it many times. So, finding one of these is a real plus in your patterning program.

During scouting, you will find examples of all three scrape types as you follow rub lines. *Seldom will you find a scrape without a rub line associated with it.* So, it is a good

Scrapes are just one of several types of buck sign that are used to clue us in to the big picture of buck movements and behavior in an area. Ideally you will combine sign analysis with actual sightings to get a feel for what truly is going on.

idea to mark scrapes, coloring them by type, on your field map as you follow rub lines. If you are using a GPS device to record such locations, it might be worth the money to get one with specific symbols or codes that can be used to identify such finds. Combining scrapes and rubs on your maps and aerial photos really will help you fill in the picture for patterning deer movements.

Your next priority is to assess *when* scrapes were made. It is a good idea, as with rubs, to attempt to determine the general time frame in which they were established, because this provides clues as to local deer patterns at various points the previous season. (We are assuming, for purposes of discussion, that you have found the scrapes during a post-season scouting trip.) A scrape covered by several layers of leaves, each of which obviously fell at a different time, probably means the scrape was made quite early in the fall, most likely the pre-rut. Some tree species shed their leaves far earlier than others, and the presence of such litter beneath layers of other types of leaves (from later-dropping varieties) can give the careful deer scout valuable insight into scrape timing. It even can give some indication of whether or not the scrape was worked repeatedly through the fall.

You probably will find that some scrapes show little buildup of leaves and other forest debris, even in mid-winter. If you locate a scrape with only a few leaves in it, but showing no sign of being worked recently, it most likely was made (or last worked) sometime *after* the bulk of the trees shed their leaves. Some scrapes even can be worked well into spring, even though all breeding has ended. These scrapes are the ones being used at the tail end of deer season, and more often than not are associated with late-winter cover or feeding areas.

You also should record information about the tracks you find within scrapes. The relative size of tracks should be noted, but be careful! Because does make scrapes and regularly visit those made by bucks, it is easy to confuse the tracks of mature does and young bucks.

Once you have covered your entire hunting area with thorough scouting trips based on study of your topographic maps and aerial photos, you have completed the first phase of patterning. You now have a map chock full of little marks and symbols which, when studied, will tell you a great deal about general deer movement in the area, as well as what certain bucks are doing. Patterning is not a single year's process, however; you will accumulate more information each year, eventually working out the movement pattern and timing of activity over the entire hunting area. This information, when combined with observations of deer during the summer and hunting season, will begin to show you a coherent pattern that makes perfect sense from the viewpoint of the local whitetails.

In the following chapter, we will learn to identify three of the most important features of any mature buck's home range: his staging areas, his sanctuaries and the travel corridors linking these special places to the rest of his world. Once we have these key bits of information in hand, we will be closing in on a strong hunting plan for putting a trophy on the wall.

Chapter 7

Staging Areas, Travel Corridors & Buck Sanctuaries

Other than being asked about the actual patterning of whitetails, the question we most often hear is how to locate and identify several critical portions of a deer's home range: staging areas, travel corridors and bedding areas, including sanctuaries. How deer utilize these major parts of their range while feeding, breeding and resting plays a major role in determining when and where we will hunt throughout the season.

Many magazine articles have been devoted to these important parts of the deer's home turf in recent years. However, most whitetail hunters still would admit to not knowing as much about these places as they would like. With that in mind, let us now take an in-depth look at how the process of locating staging areas, travel corridors, beds and sanctuaries is done.

Staging Areas

You will harvest more mature bucks adjacent to (though not necessarily within) staging areas than in other portions of a buck's home range. Thus, it is essential that you understand where staging areas can be found.

The staging area is the center of social activity for whitetails in a given area. It is the place where deer congregate prior to venturing onto more exposed feeding grounds. Because whitetails are basically nocturnal in their movements, a staging area becomes a place for them to "kill time" prior to moving out to feed. Thus, staging areas are used a great deal in late afternoon, while deer wait for dim light that gives them a greater feeling of security in the more open feeding area.

The staging area also is a junction of travel corridors that lead from many different home ranges, centers of activity (core areas) and bedding areas, including sanctuaries. Because so much activity is being funneled into a single place, the staging area offers you your best odds of scoring on a good buck — provided, of course, that you hunt it properly.

Before you can do that, or course, you must find the staging area. As noted, they are most common on the prevailing downwind side of feeding areas. With such a setup, deer can move from their beds to the staging area (following a travel corridor) and then stand motionless for several minutes or longer, in order to determine if any danger awaits in the relatively open feeding area itself.

Obviously, we should begin our search for staging areas by looking at our topographic maps and aerial photos. As we do so, we will be able to identify likely places for such areas, based on a number of factors, though not every one of the staging areas on a given piece of land will be active at the same time. A good understanding of deer forages and feeding habits, as well as continuous monitoring of what the deer are doing, will pay off here.

Ideally, we will begin our analysis of staging areas in the spring. That's right, the spring! It's actually one of the best times to investigate deer habitat, because by then, deer have shifted back to their classic pattern of movement in early morning and late afternoon, meaning you can scout during the midday without bothering them too much. Spring is a pretty relaxed time for whitetails.

Using your aerial photo, locate all areas that might afford high volumes of nutritious forage. A recent clearcut, for example, can produce as much as 3,000 pounds of forage per acre annually for the first three to seven years.

Newly planted crops, such as soybeans, corn and wheat, also provide deer with superior nutrition. But obviously, it is critical that your aerial photos be up to date, because old photos can present a very different picture of the land. Nothing is more irritating than going to an area you thought was clearcut and finding a stand of tall conifers, with no browse in the understory!

If you are hunting a small parcel of land or are already intimately familiar with your area, it might be unnecessary to spend much time looking at an aerial photo. Perhaps you will want to skip that and go right to the next step: *ground truthing.* All this means is making a physical inspection of

One of the best ways to find potential staging areas is to locate active doe feeding areas. Again, the infrared photo provides a valuable tool for doing exactly this. In this example, the pinkish area represents an actively growing agricultural field, while the grayish area identifies a fallow field. Of course, your photo may or may not be current, so you must ground-truth the location for final confirmation.

selected sites, in order to determine what is there. Once you have identified potential feeding sites, visit them for a firsthand look. Remember that, as discussed earlier, deer feeding activity can be likened to a "moving party," with

the focus of activity jumping from place to place frequently. The normal annual sequence is for whitetails to feed on weeds (forbs) and agricultural crops in the spring, then shift to browse and some crops in the summer, move to high-energy foods in the fall, and then wait out winter by relying on a diet of residual browse, mast and crop "leftovers."

This photo was taken from an actual trophy buck's staging area, looking out into a food plot. Here, the approaching buck can stand motionless in protective cover, studying the plot for signs of danger before entering the opening.

Spring scouting allows you to intercept the seasonal feeding pattern, so you can follow changes in activity centers as hunting season approaches. But each spring can be different, due to changes in field plantings and the successional regrowth of clearcuts, etc. Again, your field notebook will come in quite handy for letting you keep track of these annual changes.

You should learn some of the skills utilized by biologists in assessing habitat quality, because this ability will help you stay in touch with deer patterns. Remember that deer eat a variety of food items, but their mainstay is browse (the leaves and stems of woody plants). Thus, you should focus your attention on this food base. Whitetails will be looking for high-energy foods, such as acorns and corn, in the fall, but they must depend on browse as back-up food. Every hunter should know which plants are preferred by deer in his area, as well as those used during the toughest parts of winter.

Professional whitetail managers classify each plant into one of three categories, which are based on relative desirability by deer: *preferred, mainstay and emergency*. A local biologist with your state wildlife department can help you learn to identify the better forage species in your area; you also can consult one of a number of publications on this topic. Do not get the idea that only a biologist can identify various plants, because laymen have been doing so for years. (Aboriginal peoples probably were some of the best at identifying plants, despite the fact that they never attended a single college class on the subject. So, you can learn plants, too!)

Here is the best way to assess deer browsing on your land. First, locate all of the potential browse-production areas on your map/photo. Indicate all of these on it and try to determine the rough size of each. Smaller browse areas (35 acres of less) are more attractive to deer than are 500-acre clearcuts.

The next step is to visit each potential browse-production area and conduct a *browse survey*. The best way to do this is to start at a randomly selected point on the edge of the area; then walk measured distances and stop periodically to examine extent of browsing for each forage species. When you reach that point, mark off an imaginary circle 10 feet across, with you in the middle. Using your knowledge of the three above categories of forage species, determine how heavily they have been utilized.Of course, to do this you must learn to recognize deer browsing.

This is not difficult to do, because deer have a distinctive way of pinching off vegetation. Whitetails have only upper teeth in the front of the mouth, so they cannot cut vegetation cleanly, as can such mammals as rabbits; thus, plants that have been browsed by deer will *not* have cleanly cut surfaces. The best way to estimate the percentage of stems browsed is to pick 10 stems at random and examine each, counting the number that show signs of browsing. Divide this number by 10 in order to calculate the percentage browsed. Then, keep a running tally of the amount of utilization for each of the three palatability classes as you check 5 to 10 plots.

Look for evidence of deer browsing whenever you're in the field; it will help you zero in on current feeding patterns.

Visit potential foraging areas each month, if possible, to assess the extent of utilization by deer; you even can graph cumulative browsing over the year. High utilization means a large number of deer are in the area, especially if there are signs of mainstay and emergency plants being consumed. Also, a sudden increase in browsing indicates that the "moving party" is in that area.

The same process can be applied to agricultural crops. Monitor use over time and record in your field notebook the extent of foraging, as well as the stage of maturity of the crop. Some agricultural crops, such as sorghum and corn, are attractive to deer during early growth stages, but then become less attractive and are not utilized until the seed head reaches maturity.

Mast production can be highly variable and requires considerable in-the-field observation to assess. In areas within the range of oaks, pecans and such soft-mast fruits as grapes, apples and berries, you should first locate likely locations of such plants on your map/photo, then visit those sites to confirm the presence of mast producers.

Even if soft-mast species are present, however, they might not be attractive to deer when hunting season rolls around. For example, an apple orchard that shows up on your aerial photo might turn out, upon inspection, to be barren of fruit that year, for a variety of reasons.

When looking for concentrations of acorns, first check your aerial photo and search for what potentially could be oaks. (See Chapter 3.) Oaks generally are classified into two groups: white and red (black) oaks. Those in the white-oak family generally produce acorns annually, with peak years determined by growing conditions. Red oaks, on the other hand, set fruit one year, but wait until the next for

White oaks (right) flower in the spring and drop acorns later that year. Red oaks, conversely, flower one spring but wait until fall of the following year to yield fruit. Learn to gauge mast crops and their effects on your deer.

acorns to mature. Hence, the effect of poor growing conditions might not be seen for two years.

Beginning in early summer, it is a good idea to conduct a mast census. By that time of year, many mast-producing species will have identifiable fruit, though most of the crop will be several months from maturity. In a manner similar to that used when conducting a browse survey, simply travel a random line through a stand of trees. Stop at regular intervals and then examine 10 limbs, using binoculars. Keep a tally of the total number of fruit counted

Irv Turpen arrowed this 141-point Kentucky buck in an acorn flat near a crop field.

and divide by 10; this will yield a *relative fruit index.* This number means little for a single year, admittedly, but if you continue to keep track of mast production faithfully each year, you soon will develop an index for comparison.

We offer this caution, however: Be sure you return to check on mast again, with the best time being just prior to fall. A good spring can cause oaks to set a large amount of fruit, only to lose it if drought conditions set in during the summer. If you do not check on the crop late in the growing season, you could return to hunt the area, only to find a crop failure. The same principle holds true for agricultural crops, as they can fail too. Again, all of these findings are carefully recorded in your field notebook, as they will go into the formulation of a scouting report and hunting plan.

Now we have located all of the potential feeding areas on the property, assessed the relative attractiveness of each and recorded all of this in our notebook. The next step in your scouting should be to search for staging areas.

Joe Hanson shot this 159 7/8-point Pope and Young buck near a staging area in Alberta on October 26, 1991. The deer was arrowed in a woodlot adjacent to an alfalfa field which served as one of the prime food sources in the area.

Staging Areas

Again, to find staging areas, go to each feeding area and examine areas that are downwind (given the prevailing wind direction) of them. In most cases, you will find that there is either a year-round prevailing wind or perhaps two (one for the warm season, one for the cool season). Because this part of our scouting is being done in the warm season, we will want to search for staging areas downwind of the prevailing summer breezes.

Obviously, unless your area has a single prevailing wind, you should not expect to find such autumn sign as rubs or scrapes in a warm-season staging area. Rather, such a place will be marked by a high number of deer pellets and ample sign of what we call "recreational browsing." This feeding occurs because the deer in the staging area are on their feet, and whitetails are naturally inclined to browse while active. Because of this, staging areas tend to receive heavier browsing pressure than do other "cover" areas. *Indications of heavy browsing, along with numerous pellet groups, are sure signs that you have found a staging area.* Mark its location on your map/photo, then start looking for the next one.

Late winter is the best time for initially locating feeding and staging areas that are used in the fall. Areas you suspect will be used heavily during hunting season must be examined, in most cases, with *last* year in mind. Search for such rutting sign as old rubs, signposts and scrapes, along with numerous pellet groups, which tend to last well into late winter. Once you have located such places, you need return only once each year, during late summer, to assess that year's outlook for mast/crop production. If your forage surveys do *not* show much promise for the coming hunting season, you can anticipate a shift in deer activity toward areas with higher browse production.

After two or more years of this type of analysis, you will be able to anticipate deer movement in your area long before the deer themselves "decide" what they are going to do. It is amazing the number of hunters who report mysterious shifts in the areas favored by their deer. "Our deer are unpredictable," these hunters say. "One week they are in one area, and the next week they are in another. There's just no figuring them out!" Well, what such hunters actually are admitting is that they have not been very observant and have not done their homework.

We have yet to see a whitetail do anything that was not completely logical; some folks just do not understand *deer* logic. The trick is always to ask yourself: "If I were a whitetail buck, what would I do to avoid being detected by a human?" In most cases, if you give it some common sense thought, you will come to the same conclusion.

Travel Corridors

The first time James discussed the concept of travel corridors was in an early issue of *North American WHITE-TAIL* magazine. Later, in 1991, he followed that up with a more detailed discussion in his book, *A Practical Guide To Producing and Harvesting White-tailed Deer.* As you probably will recall, we touched upon the basic keys of finding and identifying travel corridors in Chapter 6. Now it is time to talk about these important features in greater detail.

In order to understand travel corridors, as well as the relevance of bedding areas and sanctuaries, we must establish a clear understanding of how bucks differ from does. With whitetails, as with many other mammals, the behavioral differences between males and females are so pronounced that for all practical purposes, we might as well consider them to be separate species. Numerous studies of mammalian behavior have shown that males and females tend to select different habitats and have different movement patterns. As noted in Chapter 2, this minimizes competition for prime habitat between the sexes, especially during the reproductive and young-rearing periods.

Natural selection is often talked about, but is rarely well understood by the general public. Most often, we hear folks speaking of it as "survival of the fittest," suggesting that the victory goes to those individuals that can outfight, outrun, outfly or even outthink others of their species. Although these abilities certainly aid in survival, the "name of the game" in natural selection is *outreproducing* your competitors. The individual producing the most surviving offspring gains a greater place in succeeding generations, with its genes representing a larger proportion of the overall genetic pool.

In essence, the male that produces the most offspring, regardless of how long *he* lives, is the most "successful"

Bucks use travel corridors to move from sanctuaries to staging and then feeding areas. Buck sign along these routes can be scarce; however, travel corridors are among the best places to set up for a chance at a real trophy buck.

---

male in the population. Likewise, the female producing the most young is most evolutionarily successful. But with all members of a population competing with each other for resources, how do they go about alleviating the intense competition that could hurt the group as a whole?

The answer is striking and simple. Males relegate themselves to the poorer habitats; after all, they are expendable, once they have finished breeding. The female, on the other hand, carries the genetic future of both herself and the male, so she is given access to the best feeding and cover areas. (In this age of concern over gender rights that might seem unfair, but nature is more concerned with practicality than fairness.)

James' research, and that of many other biologists, has shown that bucks and does occupy different habitats for most of the year, use different travel corridors and interact little socially outside of the rut. At other times, does barely will tolerate the presence of a buck, and they even pick on them on occasion.

In identifying travel corridors, we begin (surprise!) by once more examining our aerial photos and maps. We already have located the feeding and staging areas; now, let's see how deer move from one habitat feature to the next. Late winter is the best possible time to do so.

As noted, deer are drainage animals. They evolved in the forest, so they became associated with drainages, which provide better foraging and generally easier travel. But don't expect deer trails to be located right on the bank of a stream. In most cases, the trails are positioned near the mid-point of a slope, which presumably gives deer the option of escaping either uphill or downhill. If you walk over any piece of ground that has some slope to it, you will find that you also tend to walk along the contour, rather than continually changing elevation in steep sections.

Whitetails are somewhat lazy animals; they generally conserve energy whenever they can. Because of this, they tend to walk where travel is easy, including right on roads and the edges of cover. We even have caused deer to alter their movement patterns by clearing paths through dense thickets; the animals often will adopt such trails as their own. And while any adult deer can jump a standard barbed-wire fence, if a tree falls across the wires and lowers them in one spot, that usually will become the preferred crossing point for deer. Hopping over the wire, rather than making an all-out leap, saves some energy, and that is why they do it.

In most cases, trails showing heavy use by deer will not be buck trails. Because does travel in larger social groups than do bucks, they tend to have a greater impact on the terrain and cause trails to become more pronounced. Bucks, because of their habit of traveling alone or in small groups (maximum size perhaps three individuals for most of the year) leave fewer tracks and pellets and remove less

A TEXT BOOK BUCK

Here's a classic travel corridor setup and the buck it produced for Allen Ewanick in Pennsylvania several years ago. The buck regularly bedded at point A, in an area of heavy brush, then moved toward the doe bedding area at point B, in a swamp. All deer then moved along the creek travel corridor, through a beech grove, to reach an overgrown apple orchard within the large woodlot. Allen arrowed the Pope and Young buck at point C.

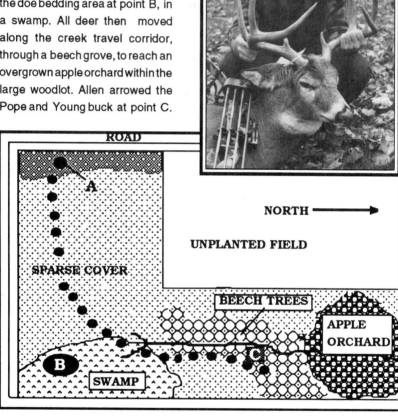

forage along the route.

The key to locating buck travel corridors is finding rubs. As you might recall from our discussion of rubs in Chapter 6, finding this particular type of buck sign is a huge aid in unraveling travel patterns. By mapping rub locations over a year or more on the same land, you can accomplish much of what it took James and other biologists many years to do by monitoring radio-collared bucks. Careful notation on your map will produce a simple "connect the dots" illustration of buck movement on your property.

In the process of doing your field work, you might find only pieces of the travel puzzle at any one time. However, by applying common sense and the information provided in this book, you should be able to fill in the missing parts of that puzzle. For example, let us say we are following a rub line that disappears on the edge of a swamp. Chances are good that it can be picked up on the other side of that swamp. In order to determine where to look for it, we will need to find the

In dry areas, travel corridors can lead to water. Tommy Witt shot this Mexico buck on a trail between two ponds.

topographic feature that allows the buck(s) to traverse the swamp. Perhaps it is a series of small, dry ridges, or a shallow area where the deer can cross with the least effort. Any feature that slows the buck in his travels and/or lets you hear him coming (as in a water crossing) has potential to serve as a stand location (setup), which we will discuss in more detail in Chapter 10.

While deer have favorite feeding areas, they also tend to browse as they travel. Vegetation within a few feet of either side of an active trail will show much higher utilization than will plants farther off the path. If you mentally track browsing sign through the forest, you often will find yourself on deer trails. Again, this often is not obvious at a glance, especially in areas where population densities are low. But it's there.

Other subtle sign also can be helpful in pointing you toward the presence of a travel corridor. For example, when deer cross logs, they tend to drag their feet and knock off chunks of decaying wood; this is especially true of mature bucks. And even though trails are difficult to see from a distance right after the annual leaf fall, a careful eye often will spot evidence of scuffed litter on the forest floor, indicating the passage of a whitetail. Learn to read these important clues. We would freely admit that not all of these pointers are news to all hunters, but it is amazing how few deer enthusiasts have grasped the concept that all sign are connected and tell a composite story.

Obviously, in areas with persistent snowfall, travel corridors are much easier to locate and interpret. This gives snow-country hunters a decided advantage in patterning whitetails, especially during the post-season period. How-

Bucks, unlike does, often bed a considerable distance from their feeding areas. Travel corridors connecting bedding (sanctuary) and feeding areas may even be several miles long. However, a buck can cover this distance in a short time. James' radio-tracking studies have shown bucks often travel at a rate of four miles per hour along these corridors.

ever, even in the South there are rare instances in which snow covers the land, if only for a day or two. This is a rare chance to get out there and discover something new about your deer; do not waste it! Follow the tracks you find in new snow and mark these "trails" on your map.

The mere fact that a deer's dewclaws show up as part of its tracks does not necessarily mean the deer in question is a buck. (See Chapter 8.) Nor will the size or pattern of droppings provide much of a clue as to the sex of the animal. James has conducted literally thousands of autopsies of deer over the years and has found no correlation between pellet size and the sex/age of the deer. Apparently, an old doe is just as likely as a buck to produce a group of large-diameter, clumped pellets.

As you scout, keep an eye out for tracks that are relatively large for your area. Then, try to find buck sign along the same trails.

Still, as you follow trails through travel corridors, you can learn some things about the animals using those trails, even without the presence of definitive buck sign. If, for example, tracks made by a deer's front hooves are large and rounded, the animal most likely was a mature buck. Scraping and pawing behaviors tend to wear down their otherwise sharp tips.

Also, the gait of a set of tracks tells a great deal about the deer. Mature bucks swing their front legs as they walk, so a swaggering gait can tip you off to the passage of a trophy deer. The hind feet also are frequently dragged along, leaving telltale evidence in snow and sometimes even on soft ground. A doe, on the other hand, steps gingerly, seldom dragging her feet except in deep snow; even then, her tracks will be less "smeared" than will those of an old buck. And finally, a mature buck tends to travel alone, or perhaps with his "toady," most of the time. Sets of tracks with the above traits most likely have been made by mature bucks. And the presence of other buck sign, such as rubs, scrapes and signposts along the trail, helps to complete the picture.

Beds

In few other aspects are the differences between bucks and does as evident as in their choices of bedding areas. This is particularly true when comparing does to *mature* bucks.

Much of this can be explained by the fact that bucks and does have quite different nutritional needs at certain times of the year. When does are nursing, they expend large amounts of protein, calcium and phosphorus in producing milk each day. Family units of does tend to hang close to

During times of hot weather whitetails invariably bed in locations featuring shade and a good air flow. Dense cover generally is avoided during the hotter portions of the year.

major feeding areas at this time, sometimes actually bedding among the very plants they are browsing. Bucks, on the other hand, have relatively low nutritional demands in the spring and do not bed as close to their dinner table, though they become much more associated with major feeding areas as the days lengthen and antler growth forces males to increase their protein intake.

Again, the time of year at which scouting begins

will dictate where you start your search for bedding areas. Either way, however, you once more should start by pulling out your topographic map and aerial photo, so you can select likely areas before you ever leave home.

Two topographic features important to deer are *slope* and *aspect*. Slope is the measure of steepness of the terrain, while aspect is the direction of exposure for a specific location. (For example, a ridge with westerly aspect slopes in that direction.) As we look for whitetail bedding areas, both slope and aspect will be considered.

Deer tend to select areas with insulation that is proper for a given time of year. In spring and summer, heat is the primary factor affecting deer movements, even in northern regions. Deer limit their activity primarily to the evening and nighttime hours during the hotter portions of the year. Habitats with an open understory are most often used for bedding. Rarely will a deer bed in the open during periods of hot weather; they much prefer shade. As a result, you often find that a dense, mature stand of conifers with little or no understory to block the breeze is a preferred warm-season bedding site. Ideally, there will be a feeding area adjacent to the bedding area, and the aspect of the slope will permit good air flow to cool the animals.

Bucks tend to bed alone or with only one or two other males. While does often bed in larger groups and face in much the same direction while bedded, for bucks it is quite different. They most often bed in such a way that they are not looking

A single large bed could be the tipoff that you have found the bed or sanctuary of a mature buck. Does are more social, generally bedding with members of their family group.

directly at each other. This not only gives them an advantage in detecting intruders, it also makes them feel more at
ease. In many mammal societies, to look directly into the
eyes of another individual is tantamount to challenging
him. Bucks much prefer not to do so when bedding. So, if
you find deer beds that show only two or three deer having
bedded there, and the bed shapes seem to indicate that the
animals were facing in different directions, chances are
good that you have located buck beds. This is a subtle but
important distinction. If you find where bucks have been
bedding, you often can accurately assess the number of
bucks in the social group.

As you travel from north to south across North America's
whitetail range, you find that the distinction between
bedding and feeding areas diminishes. Many properties in

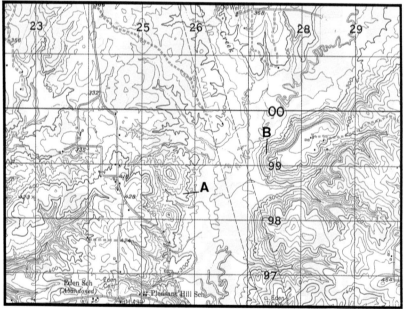

*This topographic map shows two land features important to
deer. Point A indicates a southerly facing slope, which in
winter serves as likely bedding area since it can absorb heat
from the sun. Point B marks the location of an extremely
steep slope which often tends to discourage deer travel.*

the South — especially those managed for commercial timber — have high forage productivity, so deer there seldom need to venture far for food. In most cases, the deer (does in particular) bed in and around the foraging areas, except during extremely hot times of year. When the heat is on, they move to the nearest stand of timber that affords protection from the sun and yet still provides ventilation. Again, an open understory with a dense canopy does the job.

Cool-season bedding areas are much easier to locate. Examine your topographic map closely for *gentle slopes with a southerly aspect.* Next, look at your aerial photo and identify areas with *exposure to the sun.* A clearcut or sparsely stocked timber stand offers such conditions. At this time of year, as opposed to the hot months, whitetails are seeking to increase body temperature and use the sun to help them do that whenever possible. A southerly exposure is often several degrees warmer than a slope facing the north. By lying broadside to the sun's rays, deer are able to reduce heat loss and thus, save fat stores.

Whether in warm or cold months, deer normally do not bed within travel corridors. Rather, they tend to bed in areas adjacent to trails, or even within feeding areas. Travel corridors, both for bucks and does, also tend to coalesce as deer move from bedding to feeding areas, and they come to a complete focus in a staging area.

Sanctuaries

Again, the *sanctuary* is a special type of bedding area. Knowing its location can be the single most important key to unraveling a buck's travel pattern; however, it also can be quite difficult to locate, and it certainly is the most difficult part of his home range to hunt successfully.

Although many hunters have heard of buck sanctuaries and know something about the definition of the term, we still get numerous questions about how to identify these important features, as well as how to hunt them. What exactly is the difference between a "regular" bedding area and a sanctuary, anyway?

Whereas does move from place to place as various food sources change, mature bucks tend to be "homebodies" that bed in specific places each day. Some bucks, in fact, use the same sanctuaries all their lives, leaving only to feed and breed. And because most movements into and out of these sanctuaries are made under cover of darkness, sanctuaries are quite difficult to hunt. That is why they are called sanctuaries!

Many hunters would like for us to describe the sanctuary in such a way that each one of them is easy to locate and identify. That is hardly possible, however, because they structurally have little in common from one instance to another. What they *do* have in common is what they offer the buck: an ideal location and accessibility. In order to illustrate what we mean, let us look at some actual sanctuaries of bucks we have known.

First, we want to discuss the sanctuary of a buck named "Samson," perhaps one of the best-known whitetails in the South. At this writing, he still resides at Georgia's Fort Perry Plantation, among the most intensively managed deer research areas in the entire U.S. The old patriarch is a monster basic 8-pointer that until at least age 12 scored in the 150s Boone and Crockett.

We first found Samson's sanctuary during an outbreak of a disease called bluetongue that killed off perhaps 40 percent of the deer herd at Fort Perry. This particularly nasty disease, characterized by high fever and other severe symptoms, is spread by gnats in the South, as well as in selected other parts of the nation.

Samson had been seen and photographed regularly in many of the food plots on the plantation; then, the epidemic hit. As we surveyed the damage after the disease struck, we wondered if old Samson had made it.

Many hours of searching failed to turn up our old friend,

These photos, shot within Samson's sanctuary, illustrate the features of a classic bedding site of a mature buck. **Above:** *a small pond providing water, as well as a barrier to intruders.* **Lower left:** *one of many signpost rubs within a few yards of the actual bedding spot.* **Lower right:** *accumulated droppings, clearly showing a pattern of sustained use.*

and our spirits were low. Then, one afternoon, we decided to search a swampy portion of the property, to see if any more deer had succumbed there. (Whitetails inflicted with bluetongue seek water, in order to cool off from the effects of the fever.) At the head of one of the many drainages on the property, we came to an area so dense with vegetation that we had to crawl through it on hands and knees.

Suddenly, we broke out into a small clearing surrounding a pool of water approximately 25 feet in diameter. There, in an area no larger than the average house, we found piles of fresh droppings, numerous signpost rubs and very large tracks. We even found where a big deer had regularly bedded. Leading away from this "bedroom" were three major trails, each heading in a different direction.

This infrared aerial photo taken of Fort Perry presents the various elements of Samson's life in vivid color. Important features are: sanctuary (arrow); travel corridor (A) leading from sanctuary; (B) staging area; and (C) prime feeding area.

Could this be evidence that Samson still was alive?

Late that evening, we observed a gaunt old buck emerging from the sanctuary to feed for the first time in days. No more than 300 yards from the sanctuary was a large food plot of peas, and he was hungry. That was one of our most memorable days; the king was still alive!

But aside from confirming that Samson had survived the epidemic, we learned a great deal about sanctuaries. Even though each one of them is different, the one we located on Fort Perry Plantation that day fit the description well: a bedding location that combines security with accessibility to other parts of the buck's home range. (Refer back to photos on pages 125 and 126.)

Another big buck that immediately comes to mind was patterned by former baseball player Ray Knight and James near Albany, in southwest Georgia. Ray is just as avid a deer hunter as he was a ballplayer, and he has put years of work into managing his land for trophy whitetails.

The property is broken into numerous fields of agricultural crops, including corn and soybeans, as well as areas of bottomland and upland timber and planted food plots for the deer. Over the years, Ray has found numerous sanctuaries on this land, and he has taken some nice bucks.

They first became aware of one particular buck when James and Ray found a staging area adjacent to a corn field. Each evening, they watched and videotaped several does and young bucks feeding in the corn, but never a mature buck. On a few occasions Ray did see a large-bodied animal lurking just on the edge of the trees at last light, but couldn't make out what it was. During the pre-rut, the men decided to search out the area for sign.

Just as we have been recommending, a study of aerial photos showed potential staging areas around the field. One area seemed most likely: a small, dense stand of upland hardwoods downwind of the feeding area. Sure enough, when they investigated it, they found numerous old signposts and other rubs. Mapping out the rubs and

recording their direction, James and Ray easily determined that the buck (or bucks) was coming to the staging
area via a travel corridor of timber leading right toward a
5-year-old pine plantation. Was that his sanctuary? The
scouts hoped not; pine plantations, as you probably are
aware, are very difficult to hunt.

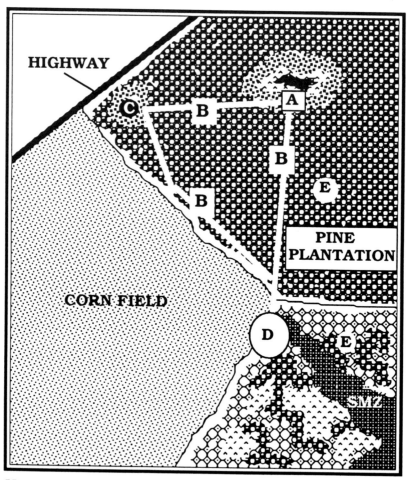

*Here is a good example of putting together all of the elements
to buck sign on your map. This buck was patterned on a
southwest Georgia plantation.Illustrated are: (A) the buck's
sanctuary; (B) travel corridor leading from sanctuary; (C)
watering pond; (D) staging area adjacent to an agricultural
field; and (E) bedding areas of does feeding in the same field.*

This was a classic *corner* situation. A corner is a place where three or more habitat types intersect, and when you find one, you can pretty well be assured of finding deer as well. In this instance, one side of the corner was a young hardwood stand; another was the corn field; a third was a streamside management zone (SMZ); and the fourth was the pine plantation. (See map.)

The trail led James and Ray right into the pines, with numerous small rubs facing them as they moved away from the field. Obviously, this was the buck's trail for returning from feeding. Where was the trail he used in the afternoons, when exiting his sanctuary? The men continued to follow the trail, along the way finding numerous single beds, some with droppings and small amounts of hair in them. This had to be a solitary buck.

In South Georgia, it is common to have stands of upland pine timber with small swamps ("sinks") interspersed. After James and Ray had followed the rub line away from the field for some 200 yards, they came to such a place. Right in the middle of the large pine plantation was a small (2 to 3 acres), wet area surrounded with black gum and brush. From the air, it looked much like a bull's-eye.

Within this sanctuary were signposts and scrapes. Visibility had been quite limited in the pines, but here there was no problem seeing. The dense canopy had eliminated the understory, making for excellent visibility. Yet, you had to study an aerial photo to know the sanctuary was there; otherwise, you would not likely have found it.

Now, they searched for the buck's exit trail. This sanctuary had two — one going back toward the field, the other leading deeper into the pines. The men followed each, but saw that the one leading toward the field was used more. Again, following rubs that had been scarred only on the side facing the sanctuary, the men came to an interesting feature. Right next to a highway, they found a deep sinkhole with a heavily used trail leading down to the water's edge. Ray knows his property quite well, but even though this waterhole was next to a highway, he had never seen it. Yet, the buck certainly knew it was there, and he used it for watering as he made his way to the staging area adjacent to the corn field.

Now that Ray and James had worked out a good portion of the buck's travel pattern, it was simple work to find the trail that completed the circuit. All they then had to do was follow the other travel corridor and decide on a setup that would allow a hunter to take the buck as he walked his pattern.

The two previous examples of sanctuaries are from the Deep South, but such places obviously exist elsewhere as

James and Dave Bzawy teamed up on this Alberta trophy buck in '93, rattling the buck out of his sanctuary. Knowing where the sanctuary was, as a result of Dave's pre-season scouting, put them into position to take this mature animal.

well. One example that comes immediately to mind was located by James and Dave Bzawy while scouting near Smoky Lake, Alberta.

The sanctuary discussed here was located in a spruce bottom, nestled in a drainage. Whereas in the South conifers tend to prefer the uplands, in many parts of the North that is not the case. In Dave's part of Alberta, for example, aspen dominates the uplands, while conifers such as spruce grow in the lowlands.

The terrain in this area is quite steep in places, characterized by ridges covered in aspen and poplar, with "canyons" of spruce. (In eastern Canada, these lowland areas would be occupied by white cedar.) Dotting the landscape are numerous fields of alfalfa. Deer feed in them until they are cleaned up, then turn to the aspens for winter browse.

Bucks can be coaxed out of sanctuaries. Liz Stonebraker shot this one on the edge of thick Montana river brush after husband Doug rattled.

The drainage in which Dave and James found this sanctuary was not unlike many located in the South and elsewhere across the continent. Following a big, mature buck's swaggering tracks through the snow, they came upon a small spruce thicket less than an acre in size. Leading into and out of it were numerous travel corridors, each clearly marked with rubs. Each rub line indicated use in only one direction, showing whether it was used either to enter or leave the sanctuary.

Within the sanctuary itself were numerous signposts, scrapes and pellet groups — but all obviously had been made the previous year. What they had found was a *post-rut* sanctuary, one used by the buck(s) as a final retreat following heavy hunting pressure and/or heavy winter snows. It would not be used again until such conditions returned.

Gary Beck beat the odds when he jumped this Idaho brute in a bedding area and shot him. Most often the buck escapes, and then becomes much harder to relocate and hunt.

You might figure this sanctuary was far back in the boondocks of western Canada, but you would be wrong. It, like the sanctuary on Ray's place in Georgia, was within sight of a public road! How many late-season hunters, desperate for a buck, had driven past this sanctuary without even giving it a second thought? After all, it contained nothing for a deer to eat, so few hunters would think a buck might live there.

Space obviously does not permit us to describe and discuss all of the many sanctuaries we have found in our hunting careers across North America. These three have all the key elements of "classic" sanctuaries. The habitat may vary, but structurally they all are very similar. Hopefully, the three examples just given, plus more to come in later chapters, will provide you some insight into this challenging portion of a mature buck's range.

We now have examined the key elements within the home range of your deer herd: feeding and staging areas,

"Samson" taught the authors a great deal about mature buck sanctuaries. The old patriarch survived an epidemic of blue tongue disease by sticking tight to his sanctuary.

travel corridors, doe bedding areas and buck sanctuaries. By locating these habitat components and putting them on your map, you should be able to see a clearly emerging pattern. Yet, before you can develop a hunting strategy, you need to get a feel for the quality of animals available on that piece of land. Now, let's see exactly how we do that.

Chapter 8

Determining Trophy Prospects

It is no great risk to claim that you would rather shoot a big buck than a small one. After all, it is human nature to covet that which is rare, and in most places today, the magnum buck is a relatively scarce commodity. We, the authors, share your fascination with big bucks and seek them in our hunting efforts as well.

As we put the principles of patterning to work in the field, as seen in chapters 6 & 7, we all are always on the lookout for sign a big buck is using the area. Fortunately, if patterning is done correctly, it not only can be used to zero in on the activity and movements of whitetails, but also can tell us much about the size of the animals in that herd. In this chapter, we will look closely at how you can use patterning to help you set trophy standards that work on the land you hunt.

What is "Big?"

Before we get too deeply into assessing trophy prospects, though, we obviously must come to some agreement on what constitutes a "big" buck. This is easier said than done, for there is no way to lay out a universally suitable definition of a "trophy" deer.

Some would argue that any buck with a rack larger than what a given hunter previously has harvested is a "trophy." Makes sense. Others, however, would point to the scoring system used by the Boone and Crockett Club and Pope and Young Club and suggest that any animal falling short of those minimums is less than a real "trophy." Other hunters might claim that "trophy" status can be defined by whether or not a buck has at least one benchmark feature: at least 8 antler points, for instance, or a 20-inch spread or maybe even a 200-pound dressed weight.

In truth, none of these is a universally accurate measure of whether or not a buck is "big." We have pondered this question for years and now would suggest to you that it is far better, from the combined standpoint of hunting and resource management, to gauge buck quality first by age, then by various other antler and/or body traits found desirable by the hunter in question.

The reason age is such a critical component of trophy assessment is that it unfailingly goes hand in hand with both a deer's physical size and the more subjective quality of the hunting experience. As deer progress through the age classes, they necessarily become not only more rare, through simple attrition, but also more difficult to

There's no doubt this fine Texas buck, shot by Bobby Parker, is a real trophy. But, despite the big rack, the deer's most important attribute is that he reached his potential.

hunt. And it is obvious that they become physically larger as well, leading to greater impressiveness in a tangible way. Each of these qualities contributes to the trophy-hunting experience to make it appealing to a large number of deer hunters across North America today.

The simple fact is that, no matter what his genetics for body size or antler quality might be, and no matter how well fed a buck is, he is a more challenging adversary as he reaches maturity, and that is not to be overlooked as a key part of the "quality" question. If we are really into setting difficult goals for ourselves as hunters, we should focus our buck hunting on animals of at least the age of 3 1/2 years, which have had a chance not only to achieve significant size of body and antler, but also to hone their survival skills and present a true challenge.

If a buck has good genetics and proper nutrition, he need not reach old age in order to produce a trophy rack. Bill Schanks shot this 4 1/2-year-old Missouri buck in 1991, and the deer now ranks as one of the state's best non-typicals ever, with a Boone and Crockett score of 221 4/8 points.

The good news is that, by adopting such a philosophy, we have removed any need to abandon our current hunting areas and start jet-setting to the other end of North America. If we use age 3 1/2 as our primary minimum requirement for what is a "shooter" buck, we can find "trophies" just about everywhere there are whitetails. Some lands hold far more mature bucks than others, of course, but at worst, we should be able to stay somewhere within driving distance of home and hunt at least one buck meeting this criterion.

Some hunters, especially those with several such bucks already to their credit, will want to use age 4 1/2 or even 5 1/2 as their personal minimum for what is an acceptable buck. To each his own. But no matter where you draw the line, it is imperative that you know what such a deer really looks like in the field. One of the better ways to learn how to "age" live deer is to study videos on that topic and to hang out with a field biologist for your state's wildlife department. In many cases, these personnel work check stations and deer-processing facilities, actually aging harvested deer (by tooth wear), and if they are not too pressed for time, they often are eager to show hunters how it is done. Looking at a harvested whitetail's antler and especially body characteristics, predicting what his age will be and then having the "true" age announced by a trained biologist moments later is a great way to get up to speed on what a 3 1/2- or 4 1/2-year-old buck looks like. (We will talk more about this later.)

There are few feelings worse than that of walking up to a buck you've just shot, only to see that he is smaller than you had thought before the bullet, slug or arrow was sent on its way. Focusing your buck hunting only on "mature" bucks helps to ensure that even if the rack or body size turns out to be less than you had judged it to be, you still will have taken a challenging representative of the whitetail species. And that definition of "trophy" suits us just fine.

What's On Your Land?

We could devote pages of this book to pinpointing hot counties, river drainages and other places where your chances of encountering a mature buck are relatively high. But again, the purpose of this guide is to help you make the most of the deer hunting you already have available to you. This could be land you already have hunted a great deal, or a new tract you just now are getting to know.

It pretty well goes without saying that unless you are just now getting started on an unfamiliar piece of hunting ground, you have some idea of the quality of bucks available there. Perhaps you have harvested or at least seen some of the mature bucks; perhaps the landowner or neighbor has picked up a big shed antler. Maybe you simply have found sign that appears to have been made by a buck bigger than what you have identified visually. All of these can prove helpful in assessing trophy prospects — but they also can mislead if you do not take a careful approach. Here is a common-sense look at analyzing your own trophy prospects in a variety of ways.

If you pay close attention to rubs, you can tell a lot about the bucks that made them.

Buck Rubs

In Chapter 6, as you will recall, we talked at length about finding and assessing buck sign. One of the most critical aspects of that process is the analysis of rubs.

Now, we do not claim to have that ability to determine every detail of a buck's rack by studying his rubs, as some other

Rub size often is more of an indicator of body size and social position than of rack size. This South Georgia buck, shot by Jim Foshee during the pre-rut was making large rubs in a nearby riverbottom. The deer had a big rack, no doubt, but it hardly compared to the enormity of the animal itself, which had an amazing field-dressed weight of 255 pounds!

hunters do. However, we do believe that when you look at a large number of rubs from within the same general locale, you should be able to get a good feel for the caliber of bucks living there.

What is a "big" rub? Unfortunately, that is about like asking someone to describe a "big" buck, and we have seen how hard that is. It all depends. For instance, in eastern Canada you often see rubs on cedars 8 inches or more in diameter at the height rubbed. Of course, this is country in which bucks weighing 300 or more pounds on the hoof are fairly common. You might hunt the finest trophy country in Central Texas for a lifetime and never see a rub on a tree more than 3 inches in diameter. Yet, in each case, a "mature" buck mostly likely was responsible for the damage...and if the truth be known, in each case the buck involved might have scored 130 Boone and Crockett points!

> *...sign of repeated use of a sizable tree as a rub can be taken as evidence of a mature buck's presence...*

It is far more sensible to search for rubs (and tracks and beds) that are relatively *large for the area in which you hunt.* Until proven otherwise, we assume that big rubs and other buck sign have been made by deer which have achieved some degree of dominance and size relative to others in that population. In other words, we all want to find a rub on an 8-inch cedar, but we do not abandon the property just because no such impressive sign can be located. Many huge bucks have been shot in places where the biggest rub was no bigger in diameter than your finger. Big (mature) bucks rub big trees and small ones; little (young) bucks pretty well restrict their rubbing to small trees, though they will check out big rubs made by older bucks on occasion, especially in staging areas. (As noted, these are places where many deer of each gender interact.)

Again, sign of repeated use of a sizable tree as a rub can pretty well be taken as evidence of a mature buck's presence, and might even indicate a location where that buck can be successfully hunted. But beyond the fact that the deer making this sign is "mature," can we tell anything more about him from rubs alone? Sometimes, yes. In almost every area with big rubs, some will appear more "shredded" than others, as though the buck used a cheese grate, rather than his antlers, to work over the wood. This is especially noticeable on cedars and junipers, trees whose bark tends to be shaggy and the top layers of inner wood quite soft. What happens is that a buck uses the lower-antler area, say from the burrs up to beyond the brow tines, to work over the tree. If the buck has a "standard" rack, with fairly smooth burrs and brows and no abnormal points or heavy beading, the rub will appear to be quite normal. However, if there are any odd projections on the lower parts of the antler(s), those will gouge the wood noticeably. If this trait is found on a number of rubs in an area, you can begin to get a picture of the movements of what probably is one buck, and you can make a logical assumption that the buck is at least fairly mature. Such odd points seldom occur until age 3 1/2 or so, and the combination of large tree size and significant "shredding" is often a dead giveaway to the presence of a deer well up in years (age 5 1/2 or more). He obviously is a buck worth trying to get a good look at!

While sometimes overlooked by hunters, there is often a chance to check out track size around rubbed trees, to get another piece of evidence as to the size (and thus, age) of the buck responsible. In moist conditions, however, be careful not to overestimate the size of a buck's hooves because of the exaggerated size of the tracks. When a buck is shoving into a rub tree with all of his might, he often slips and slides a bit in the soft soil; the resulting "skid" marks sometimes look like king-sized tracks of a standing buck.

Scrape Size Vs. Buck Size

Are big ground scrapes the work of big bucks? Or are they merely the result of repeated use by a number of bucks, each making his own contribution to the size of the pawings? Either can be the case, but it is prudent to

Hunters often see a high licking branch over a scrape and immediately jump to the conclusion a "giant" buck made it. However, even relatively young ones are very innovative in finding ways to reach branches you might think are too high.

assume the latter until proven otherwise. Often, the biggest scrapes are those which lie at the confluence of multiple buck "territories," and thus get hit more frequently, by more deer, than they otherwise would. And, the more bucks get involved, the more it seems to invite further use — a snowball effect, if you will. But while that could mean a big buck is involved in the pawing, it is not necessarily so.

Once more, track size is a good indicator. Look for

pristine tracks (no running or skidding) in the damp soil or a scrape to see if one or more of the bucks passing that point has an above-average hoof size. Then, try to relate these findings to the size of other sign in the area, particularly rubs.

Many hunters see that branches high above an active scrape have been broken off, and their imaginations run wild with them. Surely any deer capable of snapping off a branch six feet above ground level must be a giant! If deer always worked such branches while standing with all four feet firmly on the earth, that observation would hold more water; however, many bucks eagerly rise on their hind legs and maul the branches with their mouths and sometimes even antlers. Even a young buck can reach a surprisingly high branch in such a manner. Pay more attention to the "big picture" of sign around the scrape site, and you will have a far better chance of coming away with a realistic appraisal of the buck's size.

"Big" Buck Tracks

We already have noted that "big" is a relative term in deer hunting, and nowhere is that more true than in assessing whitetail tracks. What might be a huge track in Florida would look no larger than that of a robust yearling in Ontario. Toss in the fact that deer, like people, have widely varying foot sizes even within a single population, and you quickly get the idea that judging bucks on the ba-

The sight of a huge track, such as this one in Maine, is enough to make any trophy hunter's imagination run wild.

It may be possible to zero in on a mature buck's pattern by tracks alone. Jerry Stafford first located this 4 1/2-year-old Pope and Young trophy by finding his large tracks on an earthen dike. A few days later, the Illinois bowhunter set up in the spot and rattled the big 8-pointer to within 10 yards.

sis of tracks alone is risky business. Still, it is reasonable to assume that the very largest tracks in any given area belong to the more mature bucks, so tracks are well worth checking out.

Keeping tabs on individual bucks by track analysis alone can be tricky, to say the least. On occasion you will be fortunate enough to find that a given buck has a distinguishing hoof characteristic, such as a split toe or uneven wear that gives him an identifiable track. Some hunters even have used plaster casts of hoofprints in their hunting areas in order to remember such characteristics and develop a "file" on individual deer. If you can pinpoint your local monster buck by using distinctive tracks, it certainly is a great advantage. However, this is most easily done in areas with low deer densities, where individual sets of tracks are less likely to be lost among those of other whitetails.

Once more, following the sign for some distance is more likely to offer an accurate picture of the buck's true size than can be gained by picking out some individual piece of evidence and fantasizing about it.

Shed Antlers

If you have spent a lot of time in the deer woods, you most likely have found at least one or two shed antlers over the years. If you live in the right place and have made shed hunting into a serious off-season pursuit, you likely have found dozens of them, including some from bucks you would like to have harvested. As a sport unto itself, shed hunting has recently achieved surprising popularity with a wide spectrum of hunters, especially in the Midwest, Great Plains, Canadian prairies and Great Lakes regions.

Many shed hunters covet their finds almost as much as they would the bucks themselves. We would not go quite that far; we would far rather shoot a big buck than merely find his headgear.

Andy Thomas shows off a world-class Ohio shed that scores more than 90 points on its own! Finding a big antler can inspire you to hunt longer than you otherwise might.

However, we recognize the value of shed hunting as an off-season activity, for it helps to clear up a lot of mysteries surrounding the bucks we hunt.

In truth, we need not find even a single shed antler to make a shed-hunting expedition worthwhile. The main reason is that shed hunting most often is done from late December on through March, a time of year ideally suited to scouting for prime stand locations for the following year.

Paul Chase picks up a nice shed in New Brunswick. Bleached antlers are easiest to see on the forest floor, but over time they frequently are chewed by small mammals.

If you need the siren's call of shed antlers to get you into the winter woods, then by all means answer it, for that is a great time to be afield for scouting purposes.

And, of course, actually finding sheds is not only exciting, but quite educational and can be a real boost to a hunter's confidence level in hunting a given buck. Often, it seems, we build many of our hunting strategies purely on the basis of buck sign, without laying eyes on the deer making that sign. We merely assume that he is a "shooter" until proven otherwise. Finding one or more of his sheds helps to lift the fog surrounding such a deer's age, size and unique rack traits. And, if the antlers are of sufficient size to get our blood pumping, they can be just what it takes to keep us on the trail of the buck himself. Like visual sightings and infrared-triggered photos, sheds make a buck real, not just some nebulous phantom known only through rubs, pellets and tracks. Once we *know* a buck is big enough to pique our interest, we can keep plugging away at him without getting burned out too soon. We can see the brass ring!

The formula for success in finding sheds is annoyingly simple: (1) know what you are looking for; (2) know where you are most likely to find it; (3) go searching when the time is right; and (4) spend enough time at it to accomplish your goals. Reading that last sentence, you would get the notion that shed hunting is actually quite easy, and you would be right. But shed <u>finding</u> is another thing.

For starters, you cannot find sizable sheds where none exists. What is more, you will not find every shed in your hunting area, no matter how hard you try. Some hunters get disillusioned with shed hunting for the first reason, others for the second. But again, the main reason to be afield in the winter is to learn as much as you can about your deer herd in general; finding sheds is the occasional bonus and for the most part, should be viewed as such. Even when you are shed hunting, we suggest you carry your topographic maps, aerial photos and other reference materials, including notebooks, for recording specific information you turn up.

Once you are fortunate enough to find a shed, note its location on your maps and photos and look closely at the antler. Is it freshly dropped? Have you seen the buck before? How old is the deer that dropped it?

Many of the sheds found are from bucks age 2 1/2 or older — not because they're so abundant, but because the small antlers of yearling bucks are so difficult to spot on the forest floor. You can learn something about any buck from his sheds, but remember that the *older the buck that dropped the antler(s), the more accurately you can predict his next rack's size and characteristics.* Yearling bucks' racks pretty well have been shown to be poor indicators of future antler potential, so even if you find one or more of a yearling's sheds, you are not going to be certain of his chances of growing a great rack several years down the road. Conversely, an antler from a 3 1/2-year-old or older buck will be starting to show a distinctive curvature and identity that probably will remain similar throughout the life of the deer. You might even be lucky enough to find a mature buck's rack that has rough burrs, forked brows or some other "gnarly" feature explaining those huge, shredded rubs you have been finding!

Sometimes, it admittedly can be difficult to tell if you are holding an antler from a great young buck or a mediocre old one. While there is some "art" to aging sheds, the general rule is that the more pedicel material (jagged bone) still attached to the underside of the burr, the older the buck is. If you get a chance to inspect a shed from a yearling buck, you likely will find it almost smooth on the underside, while a shed from a 3 1/2-year-old will be more convex and a shed from a 6 1/2-year-old more built up.

Gordon and guide Steve Bentsen caught up with this 6 1/2-year-old trophy on the Guajolota Ranch in Texas. The buck's shed at age 4 1/2 showed the same, distinctive shape.

Also, as bucks age, they sometimes begin to show "ridging" on the inside curve of the main beams, particularly between the brow tines and the G-3 (second upright) tines. Of course, older bucks tend to develop palmation, striations, vein lines, abnormal points and other such unique characteristics anyway, in addition to a sheer increase in overall mass. Looking at known-age antlers from your hunting area, such as at a check station or taxidermy studio, can help you get a better feel for whether or not the shed you have found is from a super youngster or a run-of-the-mill mature buck (but still a trophy).

Visual Observation

With the possible exception of finding a whopper shed, nothing can match seeing a live buck for telling you what walks the woods you hunt. Unfortunately, some hunters spend so much time trying to see their bucks that they fail to locate and correctly interpret buck *sign*, which is a mistake. Nonetheless, there is little question that actually seeing some bucks in your hunting area removes part of the doubt about what lives there.

Judging the age and/or size of live deer is a skill that comes from experience. However, there are some general rules that make the process easier:

Yearling bucks look quite a bit like does with antlers. They can have as many as 10 (possibly even more) points, so never use the number of antler points as an indicator of age. Also, only about 5 percent of yearling bucks ever achieve antler spreads extending outside their ears.

Bucks that are 2 1/2 years old definitely appear "beefier" than yearlings, but haven't yet developed the heavy shoulder and ham muscling of mature deer. Some 2 1/2s have antler spreads exceeding the width of their normal ear tip to ear tip distance, but they generally are still thin of antler.

Once a buck reaches age 3 1/2, he is starting to look

This fine 2 1/2-year-old buck is at a pivotal stage in his development, and should not be mistaken for an older deer. Note the lack of muscle development, especially in his neck.

like our classic image of a "big" buck. He still will not have a huge, barrel chest or the neck of a rhinoceros, and it is unlikely that he will score in excess of 140 B&C points, even in the best of habitats; however, he is certainly going to look like a deer that would not be out of place on a den wall. In comparison to yearlings or 2 1/2-year-olds, he is going to look especially good.

By age 4 1/2, a buck definitely has developed the look and demeanor of a mature animal. No matter what his rack looks like, he is going to show clear signs of body characteristics denoting maturity: a thick, deep front end; a back line showing the first indications of trying to hold up a sizable paunch; a deep flank; and chunky hams. Especially during the rut, the neck will be heavily muscled. The head definitely is starting to take on a blocky look, as though the nose is growing shorter. (It isn't.) The eyes start to squint more, it appears, perhaps due to the darkening of the forehead area in many cases. Overall, a buck of this age is generally darker than are younger bucks and does.

A buck of age 5 1/2 or more needs no introduction and should be even more obvious, even at a glance. By now, he has pretty well shown what he is capable of producing, both in terms of body and antler size. Antler mass is usually noticeably increased over that of young bucks. He simply looks "big" in every sense of the word. Even the pickiest of trophy hunters is likely to shoot the first such buck he sees under normal hunting conditions.

Of course, it is easiest to assess most age classes of bucks during the fall, when antlers are fully developed and out of velvet. But much of our scouting will be done at other times of the year; in fact, we are just as likely to be afield in the post-season period, when some bucks already have dropped one or both ant-lers, or in the summer, when racks are still grow-ing. At such times, observ-ing body traits is even more critical in order to properly age an animal. During the summer, all bucks have relatively thin necks and light-colored coats, but the fact that they often are bunched into groups makes relative aging fairly simple. Watch for indica-tions of dominance on the part of certain bucks within a bachelor group, and you likely will be able to pick

All antlers appear massive when bucks are in velvet. Watch for signs of dominance to determine which bucks in a bachelor group are oldest.

out the more mature animals present. Hopefully, their growing racks will show indications of advanced age as well, particularly by early July.

*Holding out for a monster like Ron Hamilton's Ohio buck
really makes sense only if you have scouted your hunting
area well enough to confirm such high quality is available.*

Judging buck size is admittedly a bit trickier in the
summer than we might like for it to be. It is simply not easy
to look at a bulbous, velvet-covered rack and know for sure
how big the hardened antlers will be two or three months
later. Experience is the best guide here. However, a sea-
soned deer scout should be able to look over a buck in early

August or later and have a good idea what the finished rack will be. Although some hunters think considerable growth occurs in the last month prior to velvet shedding, that generally is not the case. What you see on August 10 is pretty much what you will get in November.

Putting It All Together

None of these indications alone gives us conclusive evidence of the exact trophy prospects on our land. Even if we find huge rubs or shed antlers from the previous year, the buck might have died or relocated across the fence onto a neighbor's land. Even if we have scouted thoroughly and often and have observed many bucks on our property, we could have missed a few of them and their sign. Surprises — some good, others bad — will always be a part of hunting season. Nonetheless, if we pay particular attention to both buck sign and the deer making it, we should be able to enter the season with a reasonably accurate idea of how many large bucks are using our land, and we should even be able to get a handle on the ages of those deer.

Once these "facts" are known, it is time to make plans to harvest one or more of those better bucks, relying on the total volume of knowledge gained through our patterning work to this point. In the pages that follow, we will discuss exactly how that is done. But first, let's come up with a way for you to keep track of the great amount of information you've begun to acquire.

CHAPTER 9

Organizing Information

At this point, we have inundated you with massive amounts of information you will need to pattern deer. You may be concerned this is just too much to worry with. But, please believe us when we say it really is not very complicated, especially if you know how to organize your information into a readily understandable patterning report. Doing so will let you take advantage of the work you have done to this point. Otherwise, you will tend to forget some of your findings. As our friend, Ben Koerth, once said: "A short pencil is a whole lot better than a long memory."

Organizing A Record-keeping System

We live in an information age; everyone knows that. On the nightly news we hear politicians talk about the "information superhighway." So, most folks now realize the future belongs to those "in the know." It's no different with deer hunting. In order to understand what deer are doing on your land and when they are doing it, you'll need to develop a simple system for organizing and processing information you have gathered.

Over the years, we have written a great deal about keeping records, most notably in a diary or field journal. The old-time naturalists kept detailed records of their observations, making time each day to record important facts and insights. Likewise, a field notebook or diary will become your most valuable asset in patterning whitetails. We recommend obtaining one of the hard-bound types found in most stationery or book stores.

Because you will be using this notebook under field conditions, we suggest you use a pencil to record observa-

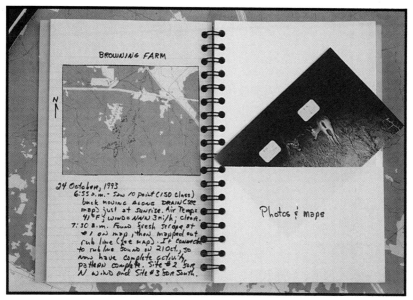

A field notebook or diary is an important part of record-keeping in patterning whitetails. It's best to use bound volumes, each individually marked for specific properties and years. The authors recommend using pencil for writing in a diary, as ink tends to run when wet. Maps and other materials can also be kept organized in a pocket in the book.

---

tions. Ink from most ballpoint and fountain pens will run or smudge when wet, resulting in unintelligible recordings. Pencil never runs, no matter how wet the page becomes. The best approach is to dedicate a single notebook for each property you hunt. That prevents confusion later, when you are trying to make sense from your notes.

We also suggest you paste either a photocopy or a portion of your aerial photo and/or topographic map inside your notebook, preferably on one of the back pages. This will allow you to record sightings and deer sign. As noted, you should develop a series of map symbols, each representing a specific type of observation or sign. For example, a triangle could represent scrapes, while dots or circles indicate rubs. It often is good to use colored map pencils, as they   are easier to interpret and are less confusing.

If your hunting centers on a specific area, you may want to acquire a large-format aerial photo (36 inches X 36 inches) and mount it on a wall. Portions of the photo can be copied for use with your field notebook. Locations of sightings and deer sign can be recorded over time to produce a historical record of your deer herd's movement and activity patterns. The importance of this photo will be apparent later. Using different colors and symbols to represent various types of sign and different years, you will be able to stand back and visualize better exactly what is going on.

Otherwise, the small-format (9 inches X 9 inches) photos are very useful, especially if you carry them to the field during scouting trips. We have perfected this technique over the years, and several successful hunters and outfitters now use it routinely. Good deer scouts often maintain file folders of small-format aerials, each clearly

Mounting your aerial photo or topographic map on the wall lets you step back and see the emerging movement pattern.

labeled and organized logically. Because our hunting territory encompasses many regions of North America, doing so allows us easy retrieval of the proper photo. File folders can be carried either in a briefcase or an inexpensive portable file box. These smaller photographs also are useful in the field when used as stereoscopic pairs. The inexpensive stereoscope discussed in Chapter 3 easily can be taken on scouting trips. This allows interpretations on site in regard to topography and vegetation characteristics.

As we discussed in Chapter 4, photos of all sorts are invaluable in patterning, not just aerials. If you don't now have one, buy yourself an inexpensive 35mm camera and carry it with you at all times. Photograph important features such as signpost rubs, scrapes, trails and terrain features to allow you to familiarize yourself with specific areas before scouting or hunting the area. If you are using

Use of such high-tech devices as infrared-triggered cameras can produce a good record of the types of bucks available on your property. The authors recommend assigning numbers to different bucks, in order to keep track of them over time.

some of the high-tech infrared camera monitors, photos of specific deer also should be catalogued and keyed to specific areas on your maps. A study conducted by the Institute showed high reliability in identifying specific bucks by antler characteristics from these photos. We assign identification numbers to each recognizable buck.

There are other uses for photos. Each buck harvested should be photographed, not only to document the hunt, but also to record antler characteristics. There are gene pools from which different antler conformations and points emerge. If your property is particularly large, say 2,500 acres or more, there may be several gene pools. By carefully logging your harvest photos, you will be able to identify each of these areas.

Among the most enjoyable jobs in record-keeping is getting photos of the bucks that come from your hunting area. Larry Thompson harvested this big deer near his home in Illinois.

Record-keeping in effective management programs also involves taking data from all deer harvested. In addition to a photograph of each buck, you also should record, either on a card or on a commercially available record form, all of the basic antler measurements. Records are not just limited to bucks, however; does also can yield a great deal of information. For example, one of the most important pieces of information about a herd is the *lactation rate* (the percentage of does in milk when harvested). This percentage indicates the health and fawn production of your herd. A healthy herd produces trophy bucks; an unhealthy herd does not! A well-managed, healthy herd should have a lactation rate of at least 80%.

(For a much more detailed discussion about interpreting herd records, see James' book: *A Practical Guide to Producing and Harvesting White-tailed Deer.*)

Finally, you should develop some system for identifying and cataloging all shed antlers found on the property. We like to write a number on the base of each antler as it is found. Numbers are sequential and unique to each shed antler. If a pair is found, we might, for example, designate them as "23A" and "23B," indicating they came from the same buck. Numbers of shed antlers can be noted in your field notebook, as well as on maps and photos.

The Basic Record-keeping System

It is important always to be able to tie observations and events to specific locations. Good record-keeping involves being able to link all observations in a meaningful manner. The key, as indicated above, is to be able to tie all the bits and pieces of information together to produce a coherent picture. We will discuss how you go about doing

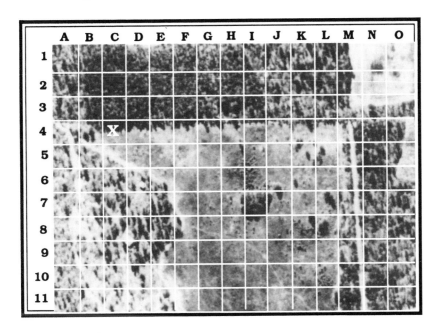

that in the next chapter. For now, let's just get you
organized.

We've found the best system is to grid your map into
quadrants, each of a fixed size. Grid intervals from 100
yards up to a quarter-mile are best. Then, just as your road
atlas uses this same system to aid you in finding a certain
street or highway, you have reference lines and quadrants
for recording sightings and other observations. As an
example, take a look at the aerial photo on page 159. This
photo has been divided into quadrants by lines a quarter-
mile apart, north-south and east-west. Each east-west line
is numbered, while each north-south line is lettered.
Suppose you see a mature buck feeding in July along the
edge of a large field. Since the sighting occurred within
quadrant C-4, we can
record this buck's lo-
cation in our notes.

> ## There are only two basic categories of data: deer sign and deer sightings.

There are many
ways to organize sup-
porting materials. The
method(s) you choose
will depend on your
situation, resources and personal work habits. Ideally, you
should have a room or corner to call your own. It may be in
the garage, attic or a spare bedroom. Dave Bzawy manages
to keep track of bucks on thousands of acres of Alberta
fringe habitat in about one-third of a room that is approximately 9 feet X 9 feet. He has a small desk, a two-drawer
filing cabinet and a leather briefcase for his photos and
maps.

There are only two basic categories of data: deer sign
and deer sightings. Deer sign alone rarely enables you to
fully pattern a specific buck; however, this book really is
not about patterning individual deer. Our goal is to enable
you to pattern the deer herd on your property. Working out
strategies to harvest a particular animal comes under the
heading "advanced patterning," perhaps the topic of a

future book. For now, let's concentrate on finding out more about your deer herd, in order to establish a hunting strategy.

As noted in Chapter 8, determining the types and availability of bucks on your property is very important. There are many sources of information about your deer, including direct and indirect observations, infrared monitor photos and shed antlers. You should organize your materials so each of these categories is housed separately; preferably each should have its own file. Shed antlers are best kept either on a shelf or in numbered boxes away from pesky rodents. Photos can be maintained either in files or

Keeping records on activity patterns of bucks allowed Susie Kroll to harvest this fine, mature South Texas 8-pointer along a travel corridor between doe bedding and feeding areas.

in an album; we prefer the latter.

As you know, our system depends heavily on the aerial photo and topographic map. It is the apparatus through which you assimilate all of your data. Using map symbols, colored lines and reference numbers, you can work out a system that allows you to easily retrieve specific information about each point or area on the map. You can stand back from a map or photo and see the total picture at a glance, or examine detail for specific areas. Then, should you see something of particular interest, you can go to the appropriate file or box and retrieve more detailed information.

Updating Records

Records deal with two dimensions: time and space. Most of our earlier discussions dealt with spatial relationships of deer — where they are. It is equally important to have a record-keeping system that allows you to periodically update your information temporally. We previously have said deer activity is a "moving party," meaning activity centers are constantly changing from one area to another. Chapter 11 will deal specifically with techniques for updating information on a time basis. For now, you should arrange your records in a manner that allows frequent updating of observations and findings.

We like to place labeled tabs in our field notebooks, as well as designating symbols on our maps to indicate weekly time intervals. When you accumulate more than one year's data, a definite pattern will emerge. This is not to say the pattern will be repeated exactly each year, because patterns primarily are food dependent, shifting as resource availability changes through time. What is a productive alfalfa field this year may be fallow or wheat stubble next year. The obvious benefit of a system that allows periodic updating is its ability to show emerging trends in activity patterns in both space *and* time.

When Randy Ivy of Nacogdoches, Texas shot this huge, 180-class buck on International Paper Co., Inc.'s Cherokee Ridge Hunting Club, it marked the end of a concerted effort to take the buck. Biologist, David Whitehouse along with James, had worked out the pattern of the buck over a two-year period. The monster's home range covered the entire 3,500 acre management area and included three different sanctuaries: an extremely steep ridge, a small island within the Turkey Creek swamp, and a dense pine thicket. Randy intercepted the buck as he skirted a small wetland across a pipeline right-of-way. (See map and photo, page 45.)

In the next chapter, we will tell you how to go about organizing a scouting report on your property. Using this report, you will be able to establish a hunting plan for the coming season. In other words, you are becoming an organized, methodical hunter of deer. No longer will you wander haphazardly around the woods. There is rhyme and reason to what you're doing.

Chapter 10

Your Hunting Plan

Well, you've made it this far! The first two-thirds or so of this book dealt with some of the more tedious aspects of patterning; now, finally, it's time to put it all together into a coherent, well-thought-out hunting plan. This chapter will discuss what you need to do in order to accomplish this task. Before we get into that, however, we want to make a point. In this chapter, we are focusing on your first hunting trips of the season — where to start. In the next chapter, we will deal with making adjustments as the season progresses.

As you probably have figured out by now, our entire patterning program centers on the use of aerial photos and topographic maps. By now, you should have at least one of these in your possession, and it should have been filled in with numerous notations about locations of rubs, signposts, scrapes, staging areas, feeding areas, bedding areas and any sanctuaries you have been able to locate. But in addition to these scouting records, you now will need the following: (1) information about the timing of the rut in your area; (2) an assessment of trophy prospects on your land; (3) a scouting report on available food supplies; and something we have not yet talked about in great detail: (4) a scouting report on what other hunters in your area are doing. Let's talk first about that important piece of the puzzle.

Patterning Hunters

Many outdoor articles are written as though you are the only hunter in the deer woods. Hypothetical situations presented in such articles seemingly assume a utopian world in which whitetails go freely about their business,

Ken Ringstad got this incredible Minnesota buck on land anyone can hunt. How did he do it? By scouting for and finding an area with virtually no hunting pressure. This 191 2/8-point trophy, with an outside spread of nearly 28 inches, was shot in a place where Ken had encountered only seven other deer hunters in 12 years.

unconcerned about hunting pressure. The reality of deer hunting for the vast majority of us is quite different, of course. In order to hunt whitetails successfully these days, we must know not only how to pattern natural deer movements but also the habits of our fellow hunters, who frequently push deer into difficult patterns to hunt.

In previous magazine articles, as well as in his "big" book, James reported on his research in public hunting. This research, conducted in National Forests, involved mapping out the hunting locations (stand sites) favored by sportsmen during deer season. Once those sites were mapped out, James measured the distance from each of them to the nearest roadway or other access point. It turned out the vast majority of stand sites were within 1500 feet (500 yards) of the access points. By marking off these "hunter influence zones" around the roads and other access points, James was able to show that, even on the most heavily hunted tracts, there are "holes" in the overall hunting pressure. This general pattern also applies to virtually every tract of private ground in North America.

Let's advance this concept a bit farther. Hunters and hunting pressure are not evenly distributed in either time or space. Studies done in every state and Canadian province indicate that most of the hunting pressure occurs during the first few days of each season. Hunters either tag out early, lose interest or simply start to feel that the return per unit of effort is not worth their continuing to hunt. This is especially true in areas with large numbers of hunters. We strongly suggest that you acquire this type of data from your wildlife agency, so that you can determine exactly *when* hunting pressure is likely to be concentrated.

Another example of heavy pressure often occurs in places where the deer season extends through Thanksgiving or even Christmas; the increase in hunters afield during such periods of free time is often called the "holiday effect." And, don't overlook the possibility that other, more localized situations can impact hunting pressure and its timing. For example, several years ago Gordon was bowhunting public land in Illinois and noticed a surprisingly high amount of hunting pressure in the area, even on weekdays outside the holiday season. The answer? There was a protracted strike of union workers at a nearby manufacturing plant, and many of those strikers, with

When hunting pressure in an area is heavy, as on opening day of gun season in many states, it often pays to be afield when other hunters are back in camp. Martin Markuson watched trespassers come past his stand right at daylight, but kept hunting. His patience was rewarded when this wide Indiana buck came within gun range at 12:45 p.m.

time on their hands, were spending each day in the woods! Such situations cannot always be anticipated, but they do affect hunting on open lands, as well as private hunting clubs.

In addition to looking at when the pressure is being exerted, you might also wish to look at the number of hunters by weapon type. Often, there are far fewer deer hunters afield during bow or other primitive-weapons seasons, and consequently, the harvest in such seasons is relatively low. But how light the hunting pressure is in bow or blackpowder season varies greatly from place to place. For example, Michigan officials estimate that of the total 1993 whitetail harvest in that state, some 98,160 of the total 330,980 deer in the harvest were shot by bowhunters, for a whopping 29.6%. Either there are some phenomenal archers afield there during bow season, or there are very high overall numbers of bowhunters. In Texas, conversely, of the estimated 452,509 whitetails taken in the '93 season, only around 15,000 — 3.3 percent — were taken by bow. When you look at such differing levels of hunting pressure, which state would seem to offer you a better chance at hunting undisturbed deer in archery season?

We both have hunted in numerous states and provinces, largely to learn as much as we can about what deer hunters all across North America must deal with in their woods. As we arrange these hunts, we must continually keep in mind the various factors of when we are most likely to encounter heavy hunting pressure, and what pressure is going to do to deer patterns. Gordon, for example, began shooting blackpowder rifles largely because in some areas he hunts in the Midwest, that type of gun affords him a chance to be afield when conditions are prime for taking a mature buck. Primitive-weapons seasons often are lightly hunted and can put you in the woods when deer are following relatively "normal" patterns.

From a spatial standpoint, you should map the locations of not only deer, but also hunting pressure. This can be done either by indicating the favorite hunting spots of buddies and other hunters or by marking off areas you have learned, through experience, traditionally get more pressure than others. When you add these "hunter influence zones" to your map or aerial photo of the property, you quickly get an idea of how hunting pressure might impact your deer.

Finally, be aware of what we often call the "three-day effect." James discovered through radio-tracking wild deer

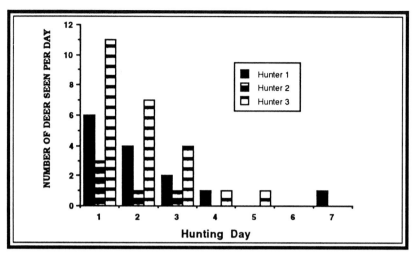

In a field study conducted by the Institute for White-tailed Deer Management and Research, the relative activity index (percentage of deer actually moving) decreased steadily over a three-day period in which hunters were in an area.

in East Texas and Louisiana that it really does take them several days to resume natural patterns after a period of heavy hunting pressure. If you plot the number of deer seen by hunters over a period of several days in the same area, by the third day the number seen per hunter drops off dramatically. It seems to take deer approximately three days to adjust back to a "normal" pattern of movement again. So, if you are going to have only a few days to hunt, consider getting there first or waiting for the deer to settle down after the first onslaught of pressure. Too many hunters think that if they don't get to hunt opening weekend, the season is a lost cause. Not so. Often, some of the best bucks are taken after the first wave of hunters have left the woods.

Where do deer go when they feel pressure? James' research with radio-collared deer on hunted lands shows they use two primary strategies to avoid danger. First, they adjust the timing of their activity to minimize contact with

humans; they become virtually nocturnal or restrict daytime movement to periods of lowest hunting pressure,
including the midday hours and/or midweek days. The
second avoidance strategy involves moving their centers
of activity to sanctuaries, which by their nature are extremely difficult to hunt. Fortunately, in either case there
are hunting strategies that work reasonably well.

You obviously should study the activity patterns of
hunters in your area — including yourself. Most deer
hunters are simple to pattern; they are in the woods when
they feel the deer are most active. Thus, the average guy
goes out around first light, sits and fidgets for an hour or
two, then goes back to camp or his home for a meal and
maybe a nap. He returns to the woods in mid- to late
afternoon and then sits and fidgets in his stand until dark.

Most mature deer understand this pattern quite well,
and those that elect to move at all during daylight hours
during hunting season do so primarily during the lightly
hunted hours from mid-morning to mid-afternoon. In
fact, this midday period is one of the very best for harvesting a trophy buck. One hunter James knows took advantage of this movement pattern by waiting until mid-morning to enter his stand on National Forest land in East
Texas. About 12:30 p.m. he took a monster 10-pointer in
an area that only a few hours earlier had contained more
than a dozen hunters! Later, interviews with some of those
hunters revealed that they felt there were no big bucks in
the area. Where there is significant hunting pressure, the
largest bucks often are shot at midday.

Now, our maps and photos have been filled in with the
final bit of detail. You now have the locations of most of the
deer activities on your property, plus what the hunters are
doing and where hunting pressure is greatest.Once you
have drawn in the areas where hunting pressure exists,
review your notes on when that pressure will be exerted.
Now, we are ready to proceed to the next step.

What Are Your Deer Doing?

Too many hunters think bucks spend the entire fall rubbing, scraping, fighting and breeding. In truth, these activities do occur, but in a logical order. (Refer back to Chapter 2 for a refresher on basic whitetail behavior patterns.) Typically, the progression of fall buck behavior is: (1) pre-rut "exercise" rubbing; :(2) late-pre-rut sparring; (3) late-pre-rut signpost construction; (4) late-pre-rut combat; (5) rut scraping; (6) breeding; and (7) post-rut breeding.

In order to success- fully key in on what bucks are doing during this over- all period influenced by their sexual urges, a hunter must "match the hatch," so to speak. That is, you must decide, as part of your hunting plan, which techniques to use at any given time. It is at this stage of planning that all of your previous obser- vations and notes about your deer herd come in handy. In addition, we suggest you contact the local deer biologist to ob-

Carefully timing his tactics to match deer activity at that point in time, Gordon tagged this 6 1/2-year-old buck on a cool December morning in Texas. The old buck was rattled to within a few yards of Gordon's ground blind.

tain factual information about rut timing, etc. (Available data often can indicate the time frame in which the majority of local does are bred; this is done by backdating fetuses from does harvested in late season and/or by observing

On December 18, 1987, considerably later than the early November rut in the Pineywoods of East Texas, James called this brute to within 10 yards, using a grunt call. Being observant and timing your tactics properly can pay off big!

---

when fawns are being dropped in the spring.)

We like to produce graphs similar to the one shown on the next page, to aid us in selecting strategies. Although the pattern might shift a few days earlier or later than the established norm for your area, you can pretty well depend on local deer sticking to the overall pattern. Supplement this information with notes taken as the season approaches, always recording when and where various rut sign appear. Remember that the rut is a sequential group of events characterized by a logical pro- gression of types of behavior. Two or three years of records from a given hunting area will allow you to zero in on what should be happening at various times.

The hunting technique you employ will depend on the

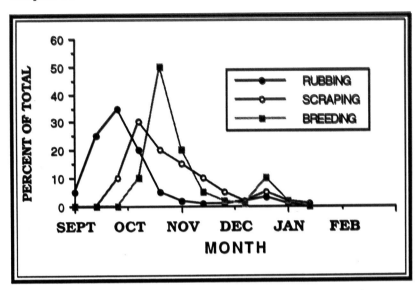

The graph above illustrates the rut chronology for East Texas. It can be used to determine what hunting strategies will work and when to use them for that specific geographic area. You can obtain similar graphs for your hunting area.

breeding chronology for your area. Once you determine what your deer are doing and when they are doing it, you can tailor your hunting plan to take advantage of it. That might force you to adopt a new tactic or weapon type if you want to swing the odds in your favor. For example, in East Texas the rut peaks in late October or the first few days of November. The rifle season does not open until the first Saturday in November, which can occur as late as the 7th. Often, bowhunters get to hunt the best rutting activity. James has started to favor bowhunting over rifle hunting in this region, as he likes to rattle bucks out of their sanctuaries. Gun hunters in such states as Iowa, Ohio, Kansas and Pennsylvania also have started to see the advantages of switching to bows in order to enjoy the best of what the rut can offer.

Where Are They Feeding?

If you have been observing your deer carefully and frequently, by now you should have information on where they are feeding — particularly the does. Observation of acorn crops and locations, agricultural-crop status and browsing patterns during the summer and early fall should be considered as you prepare for opening day. Mark on your maps and photos the locations of these important features. Remember that it is a "moving party" out there, and you have to keep up with it. (Adjustments to this early-season pattern will be discussed in the following chapter.)

Once you have information about where the does are feeding, examine your maps for staging areas identified earlier. This will allow you to zero in on those most likely being used at this time. A brief trip to the woods, for purposes of examining these staging areas *from a distance,*

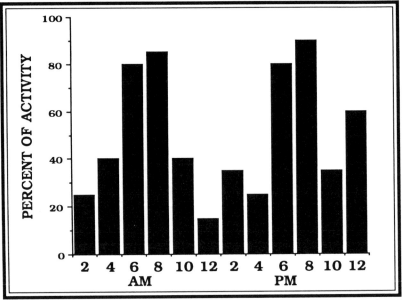

Infrared monitors were used to generate this graph of activity patterns for a deer herd. This technology allows you to pinpoint timing of deer activity on your hunting territory.

should allow you to confirm how much activity is taking place in them. Your next step is to determine how these areas are being approached by bucks.

Determining feeding activity should just be a reaffirmation of what you already have learned. As noted previously, one of the biggest pluses of patterning is that it allows you to reduce the amount of time you must spend in the field, thus allowing you to make the most of your efforts. If you already have determined the oak flat so productive last year is devoid of acorns this time around, there is no need to waste time revisiting that area right before opening day.

Travel Corridors

This is where all of that spring and summer legwork pays off. The trick is to determine which of the travel corridors you have identified currently are being used by bucks. The best way to do that is by making cautious visits to each of them and looking for fresh rubs, droppings and other sign. As the first rubs appear in early fall, we frequently mark them with brightly colored tape or even a spot of white paint about six feet off the ground, so on subsequent visits we can stay back some distance and determine if new rubs have been made since then. (Don't worry, marking rubs in this way won't spook the bucks.) A quick revisit at midday then allows you to inventory new rubs, as well as determine whether or not the first rubs have been reworked.

Another way to determine activity is to rake or brush out tracks, then return a day later to check for new ones on the trails. Of course, such high-tech devices as infrared monitors (with or without cameras) can give you a rating of how much activity is occurring, by counting the number of "events" at those locations in a given period. You obviously also get an idea of the time of day at which those deer are passing the monitor. All of this, of course, is carefully recorded on your map.

Once you have determined which travel corridors are being used, the next step is to correlate these to staging areas. If you have done your homework, especially for more than a year on that property, you can now easily identify the high-probability travel corridors. That's what patterning is all about — not *guaranteeing* yourself an easy deer, just increasing your chances of being "in the right place at the right time."

Sanctuaries

Now comes the tricky part. Although it is not imperative that you know where all of the sanctuaries on your property are, it does help if you know about *most* of them. Recently, a hunter came up to us at the Hoosier Deer Classic in Indiana, and his comments illustrate a frequent mistake made by hunters in regard to sanctuaries. "You know," he said, "I found an area just like you described in your seminar. There were signposts in a big circle, and the little stuff was torn up. But you know, I put up a stand overlooking the area and never saw that old buck."

The guy had made an innocent mistake, but a costly one. *Never hunt directly over a sanctuary.* You want to find a buck's sanctuary because doing so and studying it gives you an edge in understanding the direction(s)

James shot this big 10-pointer by setting up on the periphery the deer's sanctuary and rattling him out. It can be done.

he is traveling to and from it. That's all. We know of no situation in which a sanctuary is huntable; if it were, it wouldn't be a true sanctuary, would it? Later, we will discuss how it is possible to hunt the sanctuary from afar, so you can have a chance to see the buck without spooking him out of the area.

Knowledge Zones

Several years ago, James wrote a **North American WHITETAIL** feature on the concept of *knowledge zones* and how they are hunted. This simple concept is probably of more importance to bowhunters than gun hunters; nonetheless, every whitetail hunter should have a working knowledge of these zones and how they are used by deer. Consider, for example, the following scenario.

Bob had had a particularly tough day at the office, and finally it was time to head for home. It was an evening like any other: the freeway was crowded, the other drivers were less than friendly and the road-repair work made things even worse. Bob, preoccupied with the day's events, failed to notice that 100 acres of land alongside the road had been cleared, that an old building had been torn down and that a sign was proclaiming the opening of a new car dealership.

Bob took his usual exit from the freeway and turned onto the country road leading to his home. His spirits began to rise a bit. Glancing to his left, he casually noticed that the farmer was cutting hay. Bob loved the smell of it. Then, as he turned onto the narrow road leading to his house, the beleaguered office worker slowed a bit, so he could check out the new truck parked in front of a neighbor's house.

Turning into his own driveway, Bob made a mental inventory of his place. *"Johnny left his skates on the sidewalk again!"* he thought. *"And why is my rake leaning against the side of the garage?"*

This seems only to be the reconstruction of a typical

guy's day. But in truth, it also gives us clues as to the day-to-day life of a whitetail buck. James' most recent research has suggested that, in many ways, deer are little different from humans in the way they view their world and the changes in it. This discovery can give you a decided advantage next hunting season.

The typical home range of a whitetail is elliptical, just as it is for most other animals as well. The number of acres seeing current use depends on the time of year, geographic location and the sex and age of the deer. Some areas within the range are preferred over others; in fact, some points *never* are visited throughout the life of the deer. Also, high-use areas, including travel corridors, staging areas and sanctuaries, frequently change with the seasons. An overgrown field full of summer weeds might be

Survival largely depends upon a buck's ability to learn as much as possible about his home range. By the time he has reached maturity, he has become intimately familiar with certain places, making them difficult locations to hunt.

the center of attention in July, but totally ignored in November.

Much of a buck's home range receives little or no traffic at all. He spends only a tiny percentage of his time there, and there can be an extended period between visits to a given location. He has a general knowledge of the area, but from the standpoint of recognizing when something is out of the norm, he is at a disadvantage. In other words, he is much like Bob, who failed to notice several obvious changes in his surroundings when far from home.

Deer are particularly curious animals; they will investigate anything new in their world. They often walk right up to a logging crew working in the field, just to see what is going on. James, who has a number of deer in research pens, has found that if a glove or other "new" object is dropped in one of the pens, all of the whitetails will quickly come over to see what it is.

This curiosity serves an important function for deer: It allows them to learn a great deal about the structure of their homes range. And, intimate knowledge of the range gives them a real edge in survival.

Obviously, the amount of time a deer spends in an area greatly affects the level of knowledge that animal will have about the location. Bob didn't notice much about what was happening along the freeway, because it wasn't that important to him. As he neared his home, however, he recognized more details of the surroundings and was more concerned about how they affected his life. A buck, by the same token, has far greater knowledge of the area right around his sanctuary than he does of a distant trail used in only one season of the year.

It should be obvious by now that every buck has areas about which he knows a greater deal, others about which he knows a fair amount and still others about which he knows virtually nothing. Thus, his home range can be divided into what James has termed "knowledge zones."

These zones extend for varying distances from sanctuaries, feeding and staging areas. Their width is greatest in areas where the deer spends a great deal of time, such as in sanctuaries and staging areas, and least along travel

Hunting in low-knowledge zones along travel corridors is how Gary Young (left) and Chad Krahel arrowed all of these impressive Ohio bucks.

corridors. While traveling, a buck concerns himself with what is happening in the immediate vicinity of the trail; he pays little attention, for the most part, to what is going on some distance away. After all, travel corridors are selected so that the buck can move about without being detected.

The intensity of rubbing activity is directly related to the amount of time a buck spends in an area, as well as the type of area it is. In general, a buck tends to make signpost-type rubs within a few yards of his sanctuary, as well as within staging areas. As he moves away from his sanctuary or a staging area, the number of rubs tends to decrease, as does the width of the area being worked. When you find linear rubbing activity in a narrow band, you generally have found at least part of a buck's travel corridor. Similarly, the buck's knowledge of the surrounding area also narrows in such zones. If you study the rub lines and how they are concentrated on your maps and photos, you should be able to identify a buck's various knowledge zones.

Developing A Hunting Strategy

There are two aspects to developing your hunting strategy. First, you must determine what the deer are doing at a given time, and where they are doing it. Second, you must assign a probability to your being able to take advantage of that pattern. We have used a system for some time now that comes in quite handy in making these decisions. We assign each hunting location a "star" rating, similar to that used to assess Hollywood movies. In this system, a four-star area has the greatest probability of success for the hunter, with three-star locations being somewhat less promising, two-star areas being even poorer and one-star areas offering even worse odds. This type of rating system can be used for developing your initial hunting plan, as well as making decisions about adjusting your tactics and hunting spots. (See Chapter 11.)

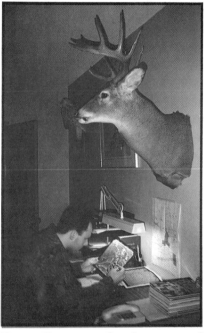

Here's how we rate our own hunting locations. First, let's determine whether or not there is high deer activity in the area — in other words, determine if the "moving party" is there. Yes? Give the place one star. Next, is there active buck sign present, especially signposts in staging areas? If the answer is yes, we now have two stars.

The next factor to consider is the huntability of the location. Is the area

Dave Bzawy checks one of his aerial photos, a critical step in determining the best stand setup for the next day.

really huntable? Before we can answer this one, we need to discuss some factors that determine huntability, which brings us back to the concept of knowledge zones.

Too many hunters spend a lot of time patterning bucks, then blow their chances by pressing the deer too hard. Understand that your chances of staying undetected within a high-knowledge zone for any amount of time are small. On the other hand, you stand a good chance of remaining undetected if you set up in a place about which the buck knows relatively little. The "Catch 22," as you might have deduced, is that the reason he knows little about such an area is that he spends far less time there. Much of the art of patterning bucks involves knowing exactly where to set up, so that you maximize your chances of seeing the deer within range, yet remain undetected by him. In other words, the trick is to find several locations (if possible) where a knowledge zone necks down in width, or where you can position yourself to overlook a high-knowledge zone without detection. Confused? Let us explain.

The knowledge-zone map on the next page shows six suggestions for stands. All are located just where a knowledge zone becomes linear, extending along a travel corridor. In each case, the suggested stand site is positioned carefully just outside of the travel corridor, taking full advantage of the wind. For example, a treestand positioned even 20 yards from a buck's travel-corridor trail but allowing the hunter a good shot at the deer probably would go undetected by the buck, while the same stand, if located right within the broad high-knowledge zone of his sanctuary, would be picked off right away.

Location No. 6 on the map is very close to a high-knowledge zone (staging area), but is located on a ridge from which a hunter could look down on the staging area. Because the travel corridor also can be viewed from this ridge, a hunter's chances of seeing the buck are enhanced even further. Thus, this is the best location of all for hunting this particular buck. He will approach the staging

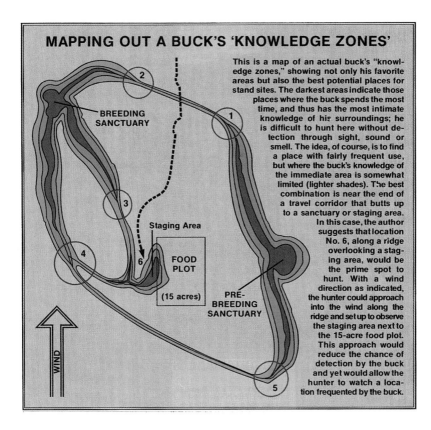

MAPPING OUT A BUCK'S 'KNOWLEDGE ZONES'

This is a map of an actual buck's "knowledge zones," showing not only his favorite areas but also the best potential places for stand sites. The darkest areas indicate those places where the buck spends the most time, and thus has the most intimate knowledge of his surroundings; he is difficult to hunt here without detection through sight, sound or smell. The idea, of course, is to find a place with fairly frequent use, but where the buck's knowledge of the immediate area is somewhat limited (lighter shades). The best combination is near the end of a travel corridor that butts up to a sanctuary or staging area. In this case, the author suggests that location No. 6, along a ridge overlooking a staging area, would be the prime spot to hunt. With a wind direction as indicated, the hunter could approach into the wind along the ridge and set up to observe the staging area next to the 15-acre food plot. This approach would reduce the chance of detection by the buck and yet would allow the hunter to watch a location frequented by the buck.

BREEDING SANCTUARY

Staging Area

FOOD PLOT

(15 acres)

PRE-BREEDING SANCTUARY

WIND

area on a trail along the mid-slope contour, so the hunter would be above him in this case. (Care would need to be taken to avoid thermal conditions that would let the deer smell the hunter before reaching a place where a good shot would be presented.) Using a proper approach into the area (see arrow), the hunter could successfully approach, set up and view the staging area without being detected. If this location were scouted early enough, such as during the previous winter, some of the understory trees could be removed, improving the hunter's ability to spot the buck. The deer would have noticed the removal of trees but would have had plenty of time to accept such changes before the next hunting season.

Once you develop a map of your hunting land and

assemble all information, you should be able to locate one or more logical setups overlooking such zones. But what if there is no such place on your property? You might decide it is better to hunt a different buck in another location providing better odds of success. Assigning a rating to this aspect of this situation is largely subjective. If you decide the place does indeed offer you a huntable situation, you give it a third star.

The final question — the one separating great setups from the rest — revolves around deer activity. As James has learned from a lifetime spent tracking radio-collared deer and monitoring them with infrared equipment, some factors have a great effect on a whitetail's desire to move. Understanding these factors is a critical aspect of maximizing your odds as a hunter.

What Makes Deer Move?

Determining exactly what causes whitetails to move on their own is indeed tricky. Perhaps that is why so many hunters ask questions on this subject. At the Institute for White-tailed Deer Management and Research, researchers currently are investigating the effects of air temperature, barometric pressure, relative humidity, precipitation, wind velocity, moon phase and moon position. Results to date have been mixed, but some common threads continue to turn up in almost every study done to date.

One of these is the effect of temperature. While it is always dangerous to make general statements about whitetails, most recent research has suggested significant differences in how southern and northern deer react to a given air temperature. From one end of North America's deer woods to the other, whitetails must endure very different temperature regimes. Northern races of deer annually face winter temperatures that would kill southern deer with ease; yet, the northern deer have little trouble under such conditions, due to physical and physiological adaptations made over the centuries. Larger bodies and longer, denser hair coats allow northern deer to tolerate extreme winters; in fact, as temperatures fall, deer in that part of the continent often increase their movement.

Southern whitetails, on the other hand, reduce their movement when temperatures are abnormally low, because these animals are not well adapted to such conditions. But then again, these thin-coated, relatively small-bodied southern races are able to cope with extremely high ambient temperatures that make life miserable for northern deer. Attempts to move big-bodied northern deer south to "improve" genetics have met with limited success, primarily due to this fact. The growth rates and overall vigor of northern whitetails drop off above a threshold tempera-

Some hunters think nasty weather conditions result in great deer movement, but this is often not the case. John Hoffman caught this huge Indiana whitetail bedding tightly in a cutover on a windy November afternoon with blowing sleet.

ture, even though such animals clearly are well adapted to life at the other end of the thermometer. So, to characterize temperatures that "make deer move" is risky at best.

We can offer some rough generalities, however. Studies on southern deer indicate that movement in the fall and winter seasons increases at moderately cool temperatures, usually between 30 and 40 degrees F., but drops off dramatically much below the freezing point. Northern deer seemingly prefer to hold tight at such "warm" temperatures, however, showing much more inclination to move when the temperature is between 0 and 30 degrees F. Both northern and southern deer tend to become more nocturnal as temperatures increase beyond their preferred ranges.

Other factors suppressing activity in whitetails everywhere include high humidity, high wind and high solar radiation (sunshine). But the most important regulator of deer movement appears to be internal. Whitetails exhibit a *circadian rhythm*, meaning their activities are based on a cycle of approxi-

> *... the most important factor in deer movement appears to be internally related.*

mately 24 hours, and this cycle is controlled by daylength (to be more exact, the number of hours of darkness within every 24-hour period). This internal clock also appears to be influenced by the position of the moon.

For years, fishermen have used solunar tables in planning the best times to be on the water. James several years ago conducted a study of his deer research area, comparing some of the commercially available fishing tables to his radio-telemetry data on whitetails, and found a remarkable correlation between the predicted "major" feeding periods for fish and the actual time of deer movement. Clearly, there is something to these tables.

Not only does the position of the moon affect deer

movement, its phase impacts your chances of seeing a deer moving of its own accord in legal shooting hours. The eyes of deer are so marvelously adapted to the task of magnifying light that even a quarter-moon night provides more than enough light for them to see as well as humans do during daylight hours. Study after study has showed that deer are primarily nocturnal animals by nature, and heavy hunting pressure makes them even more so.

The final "star" in the rating system is determined by the climatic and solunar conditions for a specific hunting day. The idea that deer hunting is poor during the day following a full moon is not simply an old wives' tale; it generally holds true. Unseasonably warm weather likewise tends to limit daytime deer movement, especially in northern climes. A wide range of environmental factors can determine whether or not a given hunt receives this final star.

Ultimately, the decision involving hunting a setup, whether it has two, three or even four stars, is entirely up to you. Again, a big part of patterning is determining your chances of harvesting a deer. If you have scouted your area well and know that the conditions at a given time are not exactly in your favor, the choice of whether or not to give it a try is yours to make.

The Setup Concept

Now we have done what we can to determine our probability for success in each of your potential hunting areas. It is time to consider exactly how you will position yourself within an area. Our setup will be a very specific location, and it should be chosen because it offers you a relatively high probability of success. The exact selection of a setup is critical in most cases, even when the area as a whole offers good odds.

With few exceptions, the enemy of the would-be trophy hunter is the permanent stand. It is critical to remember that as deer move throughout their home ranges, they

memorize (to varying degrees) their surroundings. Anything new that is left out there for any period of time will be
investigated, at which time the deer will make an assessment of whether or not it represents danger. This is
especially true of deer stands. Let a whitetail pick you off
while you are in or near that stand, and the deer will have
both you *and* the place patterned. We all have seen mature
does walk up to trees and look upward, staring right at
permanent stands (with or without hunters in them).

A setup is just a symbol on your map or aerial photo.
It is a *suggested* hunting location. Whether or not you
choose to hunt it depends on its current rating in terms of
deer activity and
huntability and the envi-
ronmental conditions on
the day you are making
your choice. *The single
most important criterion in
making the final selection
of a day's setup is wind
direction.* While seemingly
of obvious importance,
hunting the wrong spot
for a given wind condition
keeps untold numbers of
mature bucks alive.

*Determining the exact spot for
your stand requires that you
pay close attention to your
updated scouting report.*

As you scout your po-
tential hunting locations,
take time to identify their
suitability for various wind
directions, and keep a
written record of these findings. Then, you can refer to your
notations when making a final setup decision. Remember
that it is the area, not the specific setup, that receives the
rating. Each highly rated location ideally will have more
than one possible setup, with the exact choice being made
just prior to the hunt itself, when weather, wind and moon

conditions are known. Many hunters will tell you in August that they know exactly where they will be sitting when opening day rolls around months later, but that is the sign of a poor student of whitetails. We often hear hunters say, " I was over by my stand...." or something of that sort, and it immediately tells us the person in question has been patterned by the deer in his area. His chances of success on mature bucks are slim in such a place, because the deer know there is danger at that location.

By opening morning of deer season, you should have zeroed in on one or two highly rated areas, each of them determined by the various factors discussed to this point, including hunting pressure. Prior to heading afield on opening morning, step outside and check the wind and overall weather conditions, then ask if they figure to be conducive to deer sightings in one of your high-probability setups. Choose a setup that seems to offer the best odds. Move in quietly before daybreak and stay all day (unless you get your buck early). When you

Staying out of his hunting area just prior to opening day allows Lowell Deede to keep it fresh. He bagged this Minnesota trophy in a small woodlot.

leave the area after shooting hours have ended, leave no trace that you were there. If you have been hunting from a portable stand, take it out with you.

This process of determining setups on the basis of overall deer patterns and daily environmental conditions continues every time you go deer hunting. But no matter how good a certain setup looks, *never hunt the same spot on consecutive days.* You simply must give each setup time to recover from your presence, no matter how stealthily you approached it, hunted it and departed it. Lingering human scent lets deer discover that you were there, if they didn't know it already.

Putting It All Into Practice

We know you have been hit with a great deal of advice here, and some of it might seem applicable only in your dreams. But we assure you this process works and can be used effectively everywhere whitetails live. In order to illustrate the principles in action, let's analyze several examples from our experiences, including hunting (1) a staging area; (2) a travel corridor; and (3) an actual sanctuary.

An Alberta Staging Area

Several years ago, James was hunting in Alberta with Dave Bzawy. The time was late November. Dave had spent the entire summer and early fall patterning a number of deer in his hunting area, which encompasses a staggering 15,000 square miles. By the time James arrived, Dave had mapped out a number of great locations and was ready to discuss hunting them. Sitting at Dave's desk in a small farm house near Smoky Lake, outfitter and hunter formulated a plan for the week.

All summer, Dave had seen several mature bucks feeding in alfalfa fields. One of these fields had become particularly popular with the local deer as the rut approached; obviously, the "moving party" was there. A fresh snowfall now showed new tracks in several trails leading into the field. Droppings and signposts near the edge of the field bore further testimony to what was going on. (See the simplified map, which will make the story easier to follow.)

It was just on the backside of the primary rut. The moon was new (not visible), and it had snowed for several days straight. On the first morning of James' hunt, the snow had stopped and the weather had turned quite cold, around -10 degrees F. But there was no wind, and the relative humidity was below 40 percent.

The land surrounding this alfalfa field is typical of the so-called "fringe" habitat of north-central Alberta. In such places, farm country butts against vast expanses of northern boreal forests. Mild winters see the local deer staying around the farms, feeding on leftover agricultural crops; in bad winters, however, whitetails facing deep snow are forced northward into the aspen, fir and spruce habitat, where there is more cover. Fortunately, this fall had not yet seen heavy snow.

The land adjacent to this alfalfa field is much too steep to clear, so it has remained wooded. Numerous small drainages lead from the forested uplands down into the

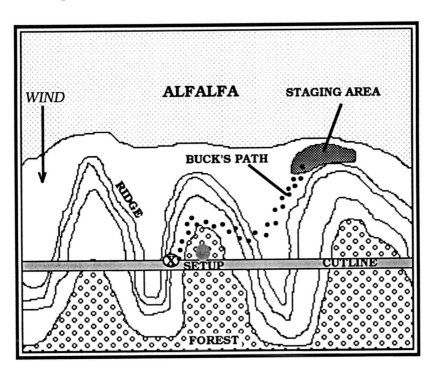

area near the field, with abundant cover and winter browse in the woods. This is where the does had chosen to bed. Their daily pattern was simple: they bedded at relatively high elevations during the day, then, late every afternoon moved down the drainages toward the field, where they staged just inside the cover until darkness came. Local hunting pressure around this and other fields was intense, as the area was clearly visible from a nearby road.

Signposts in the staging area downwind of the field indicated the presence of one or more mature bucks. One of Dave's previous hunters recently had missed a chance at a very wide-racked buck along a cutline (cleared access road) running perpendicular to the drainages. Dave and James decided the buck was still in the area and that conditions were right for hunting him.

The plan was for the men to slip into the area between the staging and bedding areas and attempt to call the buck to them on one of the cutlines. Because the does would be moving through this area very early in the morning, heading for their beds in the uplands, it would take some careful planning to get into the right position without spooking any deer. The key was the wind, which would need to be blowing from the field toward the upland bedding area in the morning.

Fortunately, that turned out to be the case, and before first light the hunter and guide slipped quietly through the snow along the edge of the cutline. They figured the buck would be bedded in the staging area, awaiting the return of the does from feeding in the field.

Setting up on a small ridge overlooking the wooded slope and drainage, Dave and James waited for good shooting light. Does began slipping across the cutline, heading back toward their beds; each stopped in the cutline to check out the situation before going on. Once, a deer winded the men from behind, but they held their position. Soon everything had settled down again, and the time was right for an attempt on the buck.

The setup concept involves studying all the materials you have amassed, then picking the right spot to intercept a mature buck. James and Dave Bzawy obviously made the right decision on this 24-inch Alberta buck.

Dave and James began with gentle rubbing of rattling antlers against nearby brush and trees, working as a team. They even grunted in tandem, hoping to convince the buck that there were two bucks in his area, vying for an estrous doe.

It didn't take long for the buck to respond. In less than 15 minutes he stepped into the cutline and stood motionless, looking at the "bucks." The report from James' 7mm Rem. Mag. shook snow from the trees, and the buck dropped in his tracks, a large cloud of powdery snow rising into the air around his massive, 300-pound body.

Because of the snow, Dave and James later took the opportunity to trace the steps taken by this 24-inch 10-pointer. Notice on the map that the bruiser had apparently responded quickly to the calling, but had stopped not far below them (out of their sight) to assess the situation. The larger number of tracks present in that spot suggests he was trying to decide on the best approach to cut off these interlopers in his area. Fortunately for the hunter and his guide, the deer decided to go up the slope to get the wind on this melee.

James was only 19 minutes into his Alberta trophy hunt when his buck hit the ground. Luck, right? Hardly. That buck was taken as a result of many man-days having been spent by Dave, scouting and patterning deer in the area. In the final hours before the hunt, James and Dave had logically weighed the information the outfitter had collected, decided on the correct approach and hunting technique and then carried it out to put a great trophy onto the wall.

Obviously, this hunt, like all others, could have ended on a less positive note. Not every decision has such glorious results. But as we keep saying, patterning improves your odds of making the right moves. Babe Ruth was certainly one of the greatest hitters of all time, but he still struck out a lot!

A Montana Travel Corridor

In mid-November 1983, Gordon and several friends went on a do-it-yourself whitetail hunt in central Montana, a region of open prairies, occasional pine ridges and small river valleys containing scattered agricultural fields. This was the first time anyone in the party had visited the area, but a local steered them to one of the valley's better hunting spots. A huge field of crop stubble lay between some pine-dotted ridges and a brushy river bottom, and whitetails from both cover areas were converging on the field each night.

In areas with limited deer cover, many hunters think the hunting will be a snap; after all, where could a buck hide? Well, they do a pretty good job of it, largely through turning to nocturnal movement after days spent hiding in willow thickets and even on sagebrush flats far from "classic" deer cover. This particular field had seen some hunting pressure, and the deer were not spending their time in the open during legal shooting hours.

When cover is limited, whitetail travel corridors exist where common sense tells us they should. First, there is linear travel up and down the river bottoms, where the thickest cover can be found. (Deer cross the water whenever they wish, but as with everything else, only do so when there is a reason.) Whitetails also move perpendicular to the rivers and creeks along feeder drainages, following the contours of the terrain as much as the actual cover. On all but the flattest of lands there are subtle dips and rises that nudge deer in one way or another, even if the animals are not strictly forced to go there.

Gordon's scouting during the week, conducted as he still-hunted the area, revealed that a number of does were working their way out of the river bottom each afternoon, moving up a coulee toward the field. Several good bucks had been seen in the area as well, but most had been spotted from too far away to shoot or had been seen in the truck headlights as the hunters entered or exited the ranch each day. Finally, the last afternoon of the hunt had arrived, and Gordon figured his best odds would be enjoyed if he hunted the coulee where the does had been funneling toward their feeding spot.

The advantage of this setup was that the river bottom was narrow enough there for Gordon to perch himself on the coulee rim, between the river and the field, and survey both the coulee and the river itself. Should a buck travel up or down the river bank, he would be upwind of the hunter and within rifle range. The coulee itself represented yet another travel corridor and was just about as likely to offer a shot at a buck trailing does toward the field. In effect, this setup gave Gordon a rare opportunity to hunt two travel corridors at once, boosting his odds for a last-minute buck.

In mid-November in Montana, the hunting day legally ends around 5 p.m. At roughly 4:30, a nice mature buck turned off his trail along the river and headed up the coulee, feeding along and yet keeping an eye on several does and fawns that had already moved into the depression. Gordon was scarcely hidden from the approaching buck — there simply wasn't much cover on the rocky sides of that coulee — but he held still and waited for a shot. The buck was most likely not intimately familiar with that spot anyway, having moved in mainly to take advantage of the rut, and never noticed the hunter watching him from less than 100 yards away. When the shot rang out from Gordon's .25-06 Rem., the buck fell dead in the middle of his travel corridor. In retrospect, he had used it one time too many.

You might question that such places exist where you hunt. You live in North Carolina or Quebec or Arkansas

Sticking to familiar travel corridors allows bucks to move undetected from sanctuaries to staging and feeding areas.

and don't have many coulees or sagebrush clumps. Your woods are bigger and the funnels less obvious. But they exist. If you scout hard enough to find them and recognize them for what they are, bucks will use them just as that Montana buck used the one described above. The buck you're hunting might not follow that route daily, but with patience you often have a good chance of catching him there. And when you do, he might not even realize the trap has been set until far too late.

A Forest Sanctuary

The most difficult of all situations to hunt is the sanctuary. Hopefully, we have showed you it is a terrible idea to hunt directly over one of them, because the odds of getting the buck before he detects you are almost nil. However, it is possible, if you have the skill and are a gambler, to hunt just *outside* a sanctuary.

In the minds of most hunters, to "hunt" a specific feature, whether it be a feeding area, staging area or even a sanctuary, means you hunt *right there*. You park yourself right on top of it and await your deer's arrival. Amazing numbers of hunters seemingly do not realize that you can take advantage of a favorable habitat feature without hunting right on it. For example, James recently visited with some landowners in Alabama, helping them not only to manage the deer on their property but also to develop an effective hunting strategy. "You need to hunt this spot," he urged two of the men. "It's a great location for hunting the food plot."

The hunters recoiled in surprise. The food plot was a good quarter-mile away — how could they hunt it from here? What they did not comprehend was the fact that deer were being funneled through the spot James was recommending for a setup.

This same principle applies to "hunting" sanctuaries. A good example that comes to mind is a classic battle of wits between James and a buck he affectionately named "The Boggy Slough Ghost." The hunt occurred in 1987, in the hardwood-covered bottomlands of Boggy Slough Hunting and Fishing Club in East Texas.

The buck was one James had patterned for years. He originally had found the deer in one of his research plots on the property, and over the years kept track of him through occasional sightings and sign reading. The Ghost was a great teacher of the ways in which mature bucks use sanctuaries, for he had two: one on a small "island" in a swamp(1 in map below), the other in a dense pine planta-

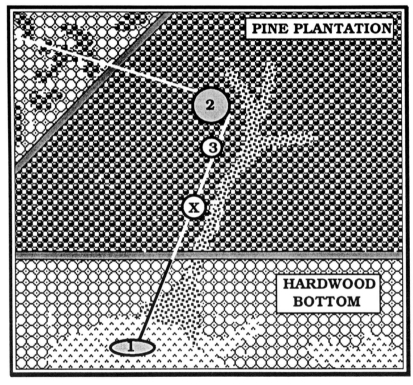

The "Ghost of Boggy Slough" provides a classic pattern for a mature buck. This trophy, 190 class buck had two sanctuaries, one in a pine plantation and the other in a swamp. Under heavy hunting pressure, the "Ghost" would just move into the densely stocked pine plantation to escape detection.

tion adjacent to the swamp (2 on map). He used the "island" sanctuary during the early hunting season, but as pressure increased, he moved to the pine sanctuary. (Boggy Slough was receiving roughly 700 man-days of hunting pressure per year, so humans definitely were a factor in deer patterns.)

The Ghost moved between his two sanctuaries via several travel corridors (3 on map). He preferred one leading to and from the swamp, as well as one leading into a mature stand of mixed pines and hardwoods. His elliptical home range was approximately 2,000 acres, reasonably small for a mature buck in East Texas. James kept track of the deer via rubs for a period of five years, though he once lost him for an entire year. By examining the buck's rubs and the chronology of their appearance and use, James determined he was coming into the pine sanctuary via the stand of mixed pines and hardwoods and leaving the sanctuary by taking the trail leading into the swamp. The swamp contained numerous oaks and little understory, however, so James reasoned the buck probably would not use that trail during daylight hours. Indeed, brushing out the trails and checking for new tracks confirmed this suspicion. Not only did the buck have a impenetrable sanctuary, he also was nocturnal. How in the world could a hunter get him?

James' work schedule and poor hunting weather kept him out of the buck's area during the early part of gun season. Numerous other guests hunted the property in the first month of the season, but none got a shot at the Boggy Slough Ghost. The stage was set for James to take his crack at the buck, but first he had to pick the right moment.

By examining data on the rut in that area, James determined that the second estrus cycle would begin in mid-December. He would hunt then, waiting for a day with cool and hopefully dry weather. Conditions thus would be right for taking the buck, provided the hunter could come up with the proper setup and method.

As the time for the secondary rut came, the weather forecast showed a period of cool, dry weather on its way. James made his hunting plans for the morning. It rained all night, but was to stop by dawn. The hunter figured that does in the area would be feeding after daybreak, after waiting out the rain. The front passed, leaving the air drier. Conditions were perfect for deer movement. There were many acorns on the oaks in the swamp, so James reasoned the does would be feeding there, with the buck still holding up in his nearby sanctuary, not yet ready to venture forth. A grunt call would certainly be in order.

Rather than move into the sanctuary itself, James decided to set up along the edge of the travel corridor leading out of the sanctuary toward the swamp ("X" on map). The wind was not perfect, but good enough to give the hunter one chance at the buck, should he respond to the call. Most likely he would approach in an arc, trying to get downwind of the grunting without showing himself. But in order to get downwind, he would have to pass through a 10-foot-wide gap on the edge of the pines.

Nothing happened after the first sequence of grunts, but that changed following the second. Suddenly, the buck appeared in the small opening and was less than 20 yards from James, who had time only to shoulder his rifle and shoot. The Ballistic Tip bullet passed through the lower shoulder, blowing away the bottom of the buck's heart and lungs. Still, the Ghost managed to run several hundred yards back into the middle of his sanctuary, where he fell dead within a few steps of one of his signposts. The massive non-typical turned out to have four drop tines and antler bases of more than 8 inches apiece!

It was both a sad and happy day for James: A sad day because it was the end to an old friend who had taught him a great deal about mature buck behavior; a happy day because they had met on equal terms and James came up the winner. Had conditions been different or had one of many things gone wrong, the "Ghost" surely would have won.

This story is yet another example of everything coming together at the right time and place to present a hunter with a single huntable opportunity. Again, the hunt could have ended in any of a number of ways, but this time it all worked out for the hunter. You always should assess your probability of success before heading into the field to hunt a given setup. Some situations offer such poor odds that you are better off elsewhere. Not all bucks live in huntable spots or travel a huntable pattern. The Boggy Slough Ghost offered only the slightest window of opportunity, and it was open for only a short time.

Hopefully, these three examples have helped you get an idea of how to formulate a coherent hunting plan from your

James' hunt for the Boggy Slough Ghost ended in triumph because the hunter carefully mapped out the deer's favorite sanctuary. The more nocturnal a buck is, the closer to his bedding area you generally must hunt for him.

accumulated information. If everything goes as planned and as hoped, you will down your buck on opening day or soon thereafter, having put all of your knowledge together in an ironclad strategy. But we all realize that doesn't happen every season. What about those cases in which you apply everything you know and still don't see the buck you want? When should you change tactics or switch to a different deer? That's the subject of our next chapter.

CHAPTER 11

Fine-tuning Your Plan

Well, you've done everything we have recommended to this point. You spent the summer collecting data on your deer herd, identified the feeding areas, low-knowledge zones, staging areas and sanctuaries. But now, three days into the season, you wonder what's wrong. You've not seen the deer you hoped and planned to see. What now? Should you hunt a new area, or simply show patience in your original plan? Hitting on the proper answer isn't always simple, but in this chapter we'll offer some sound advice about making such decisions.

Before we do, however, let's review a very important concept, one integral to any good hunting plan. Go back to the idea of the four-star rating system discussed in Chapter 10 and apply it to every situation you encounter:

1. Is there deer activity in this location?
2. Is active buck sign present?
3. Is it a huntable situation?
4. Are current environmental conditions conducive to hunting this location effectively?

Hopefully, each time you go afield you are hunting an area that has at least three "stars" in its favor. If you decide you aren't hunting the right area, it's time to refer back to earlier chapters and come up with a better location. If you do still believe the spot you've been hunting is the right one, however, let's do some troubleshooting, to see what might have gone wrong and how you can overcome it.

Troubleshooting Your Situation

Let's look at a hypothetical situation. You have located a field of winter wheat that has many active trails leading into it. One of these passes right through what you have learned is a staging area. Upon following the rubs and mapping them, you discover they lead back to a small sanctuary which includes a shallow pond with dense alders and willows around it. There is absolutely no way to hunt the sanctuary without the buck knowing you're there.

You decide to set up on the approach to the staging area, on the downwind side of the trail. Before heading afield on opening morning, you carefully check the wind to confirm it will not be blowing your scent into the staging area. Everything looks perfect. You climb into your stand before daylight and wait patiently all day — but nothing happens. Telling yourself to be patient, you do it all over again the next day as well. Still nothing. What now?

First, let's return to our rating system, to confirm we've hit a four-star location. Are you really sure the "moving party" is here at this time? How do you know? One of the best ways to check this is to use some means of monitoring deer activity on a daily basis. We like to use the rather low-tech method of raking or dragging the edge of the field during midday. If, over a 24-hour period, you find many new tracks have been made in the dragged area, you obviously have learned that deer either are using the area at night or they simply are not us-

In order to be consistently successful, the ardent deer hunter monitors what is going on with his deer herd, then tailors his location and hunting techniques to fit activity.

ing the trail you've been watching in order to enter or leave the field. If you see few tracks, conversely, the "moving party" obviously has moved on, at least temporarily. Of course, infrared monitors or even a spotting scope, set up some distance from the area, could let you determine daytime deer activity there as well.

Even if deer are present at the time you're hunting, is a mature buck among them? We know — you have found a staging area crowded with signposts, rubs and scrapes,

but is the buck still there? If your hunt is taking place at a time in which some does are coming into es- trus, the bucks will be with them. Depending on the time of your hunt, the does living in this hunting area might already have been bred, or they might not yet have come into heat. In either case, monitoring the signposts themselves and any scrapes present should let you determine how recently they have been used. As noted in Chapter 6, if you are seri- ous about judging the age of signpost and rub activ- ity, take photos of some and keep them in your records. Return periodi- cally to check out the buck sign in your area, to

Ohio hunter Greg White shows off 156-point trophy buck that was the result of serious scouting. Greg continually is checking all of his areas for deer activity.

see how their condition compares to that of the known-age signs in your photos. Also, each type of tree shows aging in a different way; the inner wood can tell you a lot about how long it has been since the sign was made. Try making some rubs of your own and you'll see what we mean. Again, photos of each stage of aging can be used as your standards for comparison.

Is the situation truly huntable? Or, have you merely convinced yourself to hunt there, based on illogical reasons? Often, hunters set up in a spot not because it is the actual best location, but because it is the best they have been able to find without devoting much time or brainpower to scouting. But perhaps more hunters err by not paying attention to the wind than for any other reason. As we have noted, hunters all across North America are notorious for deciding in August where they will be sitting on opening day of the season in the fall. To such a hunter, it wouldn't matter if a 30 mile-per-hour wind was blowing his scent right into the area where he thinks the deer are; after all, that's "his" stand!

Obviously, another major point to consider is the effect other hunters could be having on the deer you're hunting. Even if you're in the right place, there might be so many other humans in the woods that the deer are experiencing what we call "invasion shock." Then deer rapidly relocate to nearby sanctuaries or hole up in inaccessible/unhuntable cover, waiting for darkness or other times when they feel the threat from humans is minimal before they move.

Another question to ask yourself is whether or not you have picked a hunting setup that lets you get the deer before he realizes you're there. Again, it is best, whenever possible, to position yourself in a low-knowledge zone, such as a travel corridor, so that you can hunt for the maximum amount of time without being detected by the deer. Hunters often are "made" by their quarry without ever even knowing it. James saw a classic case of this while conducting a study of hunter behavior in the Pineywoods of East Texas. Using binoculars to observe fellow hunters from a safe distance, James was able to witness a great example of what *not* to do to shoot a buck.

The hunter arrived at his ladder stand just at daylight. The amount of noise he made getting into it was enough to alert even the bark on the trees, James recalls. The hunter's stand gave him a view of a nearby food plot, but by the time he had settled himself in for the morning, it was 8 a.m.

An hour later, James saw a young buck approach the food plot via a strip of trees left standing along a small stream winding through the clearcut. The deer stopped before getting into the open and stood motionless for almost an hour, watching for danger. Finally, the hunter in the ladder stand coughed; the buck simply put it in reverse and backed away. At 10 a.m. the hunter climbed down from his stand and went home. James figures he told his buddies the deer just weren't moving that morning. Could that guy have been you?

Of course, it is critical that you be hunting a place where deer are active, and at the time(s) they are active. If you have determined that, for whatever reason (pressure, moon, etc.) the deer are

More big bucks would be harvested if hunters only spent more hours on stand. James Hajas arrowed this Pennsylvania buck at 10:15 a.m.

largely nocturnal, try concentrating your efforts more during the midday hours. A full moon often results in nighttime and noontime movement; an early-late pattern of pressure does much the same. If the dim-light "prime" hours aren't working, perhaps you shouldn't even go afield until mid-morning. Your chances of being alert when a buck comes by at noon or so will be much higher. But we always advise hunters with the full day available to them to be afield every second of that time, as there are no true guarantees of when a buck *might* move.

Weather obviously can make a big difference in deer activity from one day to the next. You didn't see any action around your stand on a day when it was pouring rain and blowing a gale? It might not mean you have a bad stand, just that you were hunting on a bad day. *Never give up on a spot that looks right until you've given it a chance to produce on a day conducive to good deer movement.* Again, optimum conditions include a day that is comfortably cool or even crisp, with a light wind of three to five miles per hour blowing. Deer have good scenting ability at such times but do not give up any of their ability to hear.

When Do You Make A Change?

If the above troubleshooting exercise leaves you questioning your chances in your current setup, it's time to make some decisions. There are two basic options on the table: (1) adjust your position within the hunting spot; or (2) move to a new area. Let's look at these one at a time.

You should move your position if you feel there is a problem with the huntability of the setup you previously had selected. The wind might not really be right, or you might be crowding the buck a bit too much. It's time to back off, or perhaps try hunting a different travel corridor influenced by the same habitat feature. Sometimes, this is largely a matter of taking what you have learned about a buck and making a subtle adjustment to the setup. For example, James not long ago examined a number of soybean fields on a large Alabama landholding and addressed the concerns of a young hunter who desperately wanted to harvest a particular trophy 8-pointer that fed there. The hunter and the buck were playing a game of "cat and mouse," with the deer varying his entry trails frequently and the hunter always staying one step behind. When asked about his observations of the deer's travel patterns, the hunter could not specify which trail was being used with a given wind direction or other conditions. Most likely the buck was choosing his approach trail on the basis of wind and the specific stage of his activity pattern on a given day. The hunter was merely hoping for luck to make up for his lack of careful observation.

Once more, the amount of time you hunt a specific setup is critical. Don't forget about the three-day effect. No matter how careful you are in entering, hunting and leaving an area, some deer eventually will know you were there. It is extremely difficult to hunt a spot for three days without seeing a general decline in deer activity in the immediate area surrounding your stand site. You probably will want to have more than one setup and switch daily to reduce the impact of hunting pressure on your deer. Some successful trophy bowhunters we know actually refuse to hunt out of the same tree twice — ever! While you might be hunting some places that have so few setups you're not afforded this luxury of hopping around daily,

New Yorker Scott Hanrahan had enough faith in his South Dakota hunting area not to give up. His reward was this impressive eight point trophy.

there's no doubt the rationale is sound. Keep the deer guessing without making them feel threatened. There is no substitute for this, particularly in bow season.

Some hunters are as quiet as a mouse while in their stands, but make serious mistakes in getting to them and back out again. The shortest distance between your truck and your stand site might be a straight line, but many times that isn't the smartest way to go. Use your maps and photos and common sense to work out your approach and exit routes before you ever hit the woods that morning. Mark your way clearly, so you get in and get situated quietly well before dawn, without barreling through deer on your way. Avoid walking on deer trails, handling vegetation, etc. as you travel through the woods, and your hunting setups will stay fresh longer.

George Law hunts aggressively, searching out centers of deer activity, before setting up to rattle and call. This 156-point Washington buck is the payoff to this hunting method.

Moving to an entirely new area might be in order if your first choice has gone dry. To determine whether or not a move is in order, go back to the four-star concept. Even if you are seeing activity in your original area, it pays to spend part of your time monitoring what is going on elsewhere, because the "party" is always moving somewhat. When the day comes that you suddenly feel your hunting spot has been left behind by the deer, you then will be ready to react and pick another spot without unnecessary "down time."

Generally, no area maintains a four-star rating for the entire fall hunting season. A hotspot can drop to a rating or only two or three stars almost overnight. Likewise, an area you previously had given only two stars can suddenly become active, earning a higher rating. On days when deer movement is minimal, due to weather or other such conditions (including hunting pressure), you can make the most of your free time by monitoring these "so-so" areas for signs of improved activity. This not only gives you a chance to see what's going on in new areas, it lets your top setups rest when hunting conditions are less than ideal for success.

Even on a single tract of hunting land, deer activity can shift appreciably over a short time. Recall what we said about home ranges being elliptical? They do not really change, true, but active core areas within home ranges do shift, as deer move to take advantage of feeding areas. So, this "moving party" to which we keep referring is merely a shifting of activity centers within the larger framework of the home range. Thus, if you are only able to hunt one small piece of property, you still might be able to make some adjustments. This is especially true if there is much hunting pressure on neighboring tracts.

One of James' past hunts is a perfect illustration. He owns a small farm of around 200 acres in East Texas, an area of small farms and timberlands. His neighbors have tracts ranging from 300 to 800 acres, and on opening day of gun season, it can sound as though a small war has broken out in the surrounding woods. James became concerned that most of the bucks spending at least part of their time on his land were being killed by neighbors and their hunting buddies, but that turned out not to be true. After placing infrared-triggered cameras on his property, James was surprised to see that by the middle of gun season his land actually had a ratio of two bucks for every doe! Everyone around was pounding the bucks, but James had had no real hunting pressure on his farm, and the bucks had relocated there to find relief. Without doing anything more than giving the bucks a place to hide,

James had dramatically improved the trophy prospects on his land in a few short weeks! Judiciously selecting stand setups on the edge of his farm, he was able to harvest a beautiful non-typical scoring in the 160 class on the B&C

Vincent and Rebecca Hernandez hunt just 80 acres in Texas, but this big buck moved onto their property because of pressure on surrounding ranches, illustrating pressure can be positive.

system. This happened even as James' neighbors claimed the entire area was "shot out."

The way to monitor changes in activity on a single property is similar to that used for multiple properties. Instead of locating the "moving party" by checking on activity all over the countryside, you obviously must wait for the deer to come to you. Most hunters who are restricted to just one property share some deer with their neighbors; unless game fences separate two tracts, the animals obviously come and go as they please, in response to a variety of factors. Keeping records of various deer sign, as well as actual sightings, will give you a good idea of when the "party" has moved onto your hunting land. When it does, you might not have long to take advantage of the fact, so it pays to stay abreast of changing conditions.

We are well aware that there are significant differences in how whitetails in various regions move on a daily basis. The differences are not due to the animals themselves, but to the places in which they live. We each receive numerous phone calls from hunters who have just read articles about how to hunt the classic pattern: setting up in locations somewhere between well-defined bedding and feeding areas. "We just don't see that kind of pattern where I hunt," the caller usually will complain, and often he's not joking. Where deer have a variety of food sources on hand — a Southern clearcut, for example, or maybe a Midwest woodlot surrounded by fields — there sometimes are no major differences between where a deer feeds and where it rests. The deer simply need not move far each day (or night) in order to take care of their basic requirements.

We would not suggest that it is easy to pattern deer living in an 8-year-old Georgia clearcut or a 700-acre Iowa corn field with stalks taller than your head. In these special situations, the world of a deer is at least seasonally miniaturized, and that puts special demands on the hunter's knowledge of the land if he is to score. Careful attention to subtle detail is the key, and that is most easily achieved if a specific area is hunted year after year. Keep those maps and photos handy, and keep recording what you find, even if it makes no sense at the time. Sooner or later, it will add up, and that little light will flash on.

Anticipating Changes

Perhaps the best thing about our suggested system of patterning is that you can develop a wealth of information about your deer herd over several years. This lets you tap into the seasonal changes that occur, ultimately giving you the ability (we hope) to make your move before the deer do — to anticipate their seasonal shifts and be ready for the benefits those changes can bring you. For example, if you have been monitoring acorn production on your land and realize the mast crop is about gone for the year, you can anticipate that the deer will do what they did the last time that occurred: move to a specific crop type in a nearby field. You thus can be in place and pretty well set up on the logical trails to take advantage of that shift, and you can do it as soon as the deer themselves make the change.

You also can gauge buck movements and rutting activity if you pay close attention to what is going on with your doe groups. By keeping notes on when the members of various matriarchal units come into estrus each fall, you can annually predict within a few days when the dominant does will be receptive to bucks. By situating yourself in the right travel corridor, you thus can be waiting for the bucks to come courting, rather than "chasing the sign."

And finally, you can anticipate changes in deer movement in response to hunting pressure. Where that pressure is somewhat consistent from year to year, such as on an accessible tract of open land, you can make logical moves after studying the ways in which local deer respond to the pressure. The best hunters do this and get bucks while other guys sit around and complain about the lack of game.

Keeping track of when the rut occurs will tell you when to hunt closer to doe areas. Tony Mangum got this North Carolina trophy as the buck trailed does through a weed field.

A beautiful example is a late-October rifle hunt we went on in New Brunswick several years back. We were hunting with our good friend George Chase, an outstanding whitetail and bear guide who has hunted that province all of his life. Our quest on this trip was to bag at least one of the hefty bucks that inhabited the lower end of a river valley just off the Bay of Fundy.

The first two days produced nothing, other than an occasional encounter with a moose breaking timber on its way through the swamps. The weather was too warm, for the most part, to spark much deer movement, a fact that is difficult to work around when you're hunting far from home. We decided another area, two hours up the coastline in a farming district, was worth checking out. George had scouted it well and knew the location of at least one huge 8-pointer, a deer scoring at least in the 160s, and there certainly were other mature bucks there as well. Trying that spot would give us a look at some new land and would give the original river valley a chance to cool off for at least a day.

As it turns out, the plan was good. Nothing was shot at the farmland spot, but several deer were seen. The three of us then turned and went back south to the first spot, and only a couple of hours later, Gordon shot a 4-1/2-year-old 8-pointer with a live weight of 300 pounds. The deer was nonchalantly feeding in a big clearcut on the fourth afternoon of gun season, a bit farther into the valley than other hunters had been going. Bothering to hunt beyond the river, rather than stopping on the near side, gave Gordon a chance to shoot a trophy deer.

We've thrown a great deal at you in these pages. The system outlined here hopefully will put you into position to take a big buck next season, and to see more deer overall. Still, we must warn you that a couple of sticking points keep many well-intended hunters from ever realizing their hopes of consistent success: (1) an unwillingness to apply themselves to the job; and (2) a lack of aggressiveness in hunting. Let's examine these more closely, for it is critical that you not let either of them stop you.

Nobody can become good at deer hunting unless he or she truly wants to do so. The concepts we've discussed in this book are merely tools to use to make the most of your available hunting time. If you love deer hunting and want to become even better at it, you have to make that your goal, not an afterthought. Again, we realize free time is not that abundant, so it takes dedication to do these things.

Secondly, don't be afraid of the deer. Some hunters act as though they are, and perhaps that is what keeps them

If you can get away from hunting pressure, it is often possible to find mature bucks feeding in daylight hours before the rut kicks off. Gordon shot this New Brunswick brute in a clearcut in late October.

on the edge of that big field when the really good spots are back in the woods a ways. Don't be tentative in the woods. After all, what does the word "hunt" mean? It means to search for, to seek out, to pursue. There's nothing passive implied in that definition. Yet, all too often we encounter hunters who, like a guy dunking a worm in a convenient spot on the river, simply hope luck will bring something their way. Isn't it far better to study the habits and habitat of your quarry, then take charge by going where the action is? If you invest the time and effort to learn about your deer herd, you can go afield with the confidence that every move you make has a purpose. And when you get right down to it, that's what patterning whitetails is really about.

CHAPTER 12

A Final Word

Ours is a world in which tangible results are used to measure every sort of endeavor. Man has always been a competitive creature, and there is no reason to think that ever will end. But it can be taken too far.

As you put our principles of patterning into use and make a serious effort to become a better deer hunter, never forget why we're all in the woods each fall to begin with. Certainly we enjoy the taste of venison, but for most of us the reason for hunting deer runs deeper. We're out there to relax, to enjoy the natural world, to pit ourselves against a challenging animal that hopefully will bring out the best of our hunting skills and ethical values, so that when we do fill a tag, it is in a way that brings lasting satisfaction.

But what about those hunts — and they are many — in which no game is taken? Are we failures if we do not shoot more and/or bigger deer than the next guy? Does that somehow tarnish the hunting experience and overshadow the good which might have come from it?

Of course not. Every minute spent scouting for, hunting and even thinking about whitetails should be a pleasant one, and for the enlightened hunter it is. We all want to see deer every time we go hunting, and we all want to shoot a monster buck every season. But the fact is that it simply doesn't work out that smoothly every time. Some days you do everything right, but the breaks beat you. "Failure" affects all of us, whether we are professional outfitters, biologists, writers or beginning hunters.

You cannot predict exactly what will transpire when you go into the deer woods tomorrow. Neither can we. Finding out what will happen is perhaps the biggest part of why we go; it wouldn't be nearly as much fun if everything

These two mature bucks from the Diamond H Ranch in Texas were much appreciated. But the best "trophies" we took home from that trip were the memories of good times spent hunting deer in the company of good friends in the outdoors.

always fell into place. Yes, we want each hunt to go like clockwork, and every time we walk into the woods during open season, we hope to walk back out with a trophy deer in tow. But if it always worked out that way, many of us would end our hunting season on opening morning. Perhaps that isn't as appealing as it at first sounds.

When hunting whitetails, there is only one guarantee: that if we have prepared ourselves well for the task, and have chosen hunting partners we enjoy, we will have a good time. If a great buck is harvested, that is a welcome bonus, and one for which we will forever be grateful. But in the end, what we appreciate most is not the antlers of our quarry, but the chance to enter his world and exit our own for at least a few precious hours each fall.

The Institute for White-tailed Deer
Management & Research offers <u>YOU</u> the finest in educational materials about deer!

Ask about our videos too!

☐ ***The Art & Science of Patterning Whitetails***, Dr. James C. Kroll and Gordon Whittington. 218 pages of how-to experience in hunting mature bucks.
$24.95 (Texas residents add $2.06 tax).

☐ ***The Southern Food Plot Manual***, Ben H. Koerth and Dr. James C. Kroll. 132 pages present tried and true ways YOU can supplementally feed YOUR deer. Although aimed at the South, this book is a must for anyone, North or South, actively managing deer.
$19.95 (Texas residents add $1.65 tax.).

☐ ***A Practical Guide to Producing & Harvesting White-tailed Deer***, Dr. James C. Kroll. Hailed as the "bible" of deer management and hunting, this 591 page book is a <u>must</u> both for hunters and landowners alike.
$39.95 (Texas residents add $3.30 tax).

Order Today!

Name:_____

Address: _____

_____

_____

Phone Orders: 1-800-403-3793*

Method of Payment:

Visa __ Mastercard __ Check __

Credit Card No: _____ Exp. Date: _____

Amount (plus $3.00 <u>each item</u> S&H):$ _____

*Inquiries: 1-409-468-2004

The Institute for White-tailed Deer
Management & Research offers <u>YOU</u> the finest in educational materials about deer!

Ask about our videos too!

☐ ***The Art & Science of Patterning Whitetails***, Dr. James C. Kroll and Gordon Whittington. 218 pages of how-to experience in hunting mature bucks.
$24.95 (Texas residents add $2.06 tax).

☐ ***The Southern Food Plot Manual***, Ben H. Koerth and Dr. James C. Kroll. 132 pages present tried and true ways YOU can supplementally feed YOUR deer. Although aimed at the South, this book is a must for anyone, North or South, actively managing deer.
$19.95 (Texas residents add $1.65 tax.).

☐ ***A Practical Guide to Producing & Harvesting White-tailed Deer***, Dr. James C. Kroll. Hailed as the "bible" of deer management and hunting, this 591 page book is a <u>must</u> both for hunters and landowners alike.
$39.95 (Texas residents add $3.30 tax).

Order Today!

Name:_____

Address: _____

_____

_____

Phone Orders: 1-800-403-3793*

Method of Payment:

Visa __ Mastercard __ Check __

Credit Card No: _____ Exp. Date: _____

Amount (plus $3.00 <u>each item</u> S&H):$ _____

*Inquiries: 1-409-468-2004

Institute for White-tailed Deer
Management and Research
P.O. Box 6109 SFA Station, Dept. B
Nacogdoches, TX 75962-6109

Affix
Stamp
here.

Institute for White-tailed Deer
Management and Research
P.O. Box 6109 SFA Station, Dept. B
Nacogdoches, TX 75962-6109